THE HARRISON FORD STORY

THE HARRISON FORD STORY

Alan McKenzie

PRIAM
BOOKS

ARBOR HOUSE   NEW YORK

Library of Congress Catalog Card Number: 84-71344

ISBN: 0-87795-667-7

Manufactured in the United States of America

10 9 8 7 6 5 4 3 2 1

This book is printed on acid-free paper. The paper in this book meets the guidelines for permanence and durability of the Committee on Production Guidelines for Book Longevity of the Council on Library Resources.

This first book
is dedicated to
Walter B. Gibson

CHAPTER 1

HARRISON FORD: THE EARLY DAYS

From College to Contract Player to Carpentry

'My job is pretending to be Indiana Jones, or whoever, and I consider personal information about *me* can only water down the illusion.'
Harrison Ford

Somewhere along Hollywood Boulevard's sidewalk of showbiz fame, where the names of the stars are imbedded in the very concrete beneath the tourists' feet, there is an entry for Harrison Ford. Well, of course there is! Ford is one of the biggest box-office draws of the Eighties. You'll find him in major roles in four of the five most successful movies of all time. It would have been five out of five had his cameo role as Elliot's headmaster in *E.T. The Extra-Terrestrial* – written as it happens by the second Mrs Ford, Melissa Mathison – not been cut from the movie at the last minute. So if any of Film City's army of 'Stars', 'Superstars' and 'Megastars' deserves the honour of having his name immortalised in concrete, Harrison Ford's the one, right?

'Except,' chuckles Ford, 'that's not my star! It was put there years ago for an old time (silent) matinee idol also called Harrison Ford. No, I've never heard of him, either. Or not until the Screen Actors' Guild told me I'd have to change my name. That's why I'm Harrison J. Ford in two of my earliest films. When I heard the old man had passed on, I called up the S.A.G. about it. They couldn't confirm his death, but I dropped the J. anyway.'

The original Harrison Ford is not one of the better-remembered silent stars. He made his film debut in 1915, in a picture called *Up the Road With Sally*. His career blossomed and within a few years he was co-starring with such performers as Lon Chaney, notably *Shadows* (1922). As the Twenties wore on he gravitated towards comedies like *Up in Mabel's Room* and *The Nervous Wreck*. Little was written in the fan magazines at the time. The earlier Ford was just as hard to pin down in interviews as his namesake. 'He has a neat habit,' said one contemporary journalist, 'of placing the blame for good work onto the innocent shoulders of others. "Mary Provost is a great little actress to work with in comedy" or "Phyllis Haver is splendid in it also" are the sort of facts he will remind you of if you compliment him on his own acting.' The first Ford died at the age of 73 on 2nd December 1957, ten years after retiring from acting.

'If they ever decide to put an entry there for me,' says Ford, 'they needn't bother. It's there already. And I kind of like the idea of using his.' Sentimental perhaps, but the 'old man' would probably have approved.

IN THE BEGINNING

Harrison Ford II has a reputation for being a very private man, and little is recorded about his early life. 'I was raised in Chicago,' says Ford in a rare moment of self-revelation. 'Nothing too remarkable there. Just the usual. Baseball, fooling around with cars. I was a loner type. Not very active in sports. I didn't know what I wanted to do when I was a kid.'

Harrison Ford was born on July 13th, 1942 of an Irish Catholic mother and a Russian Jewish father. His childhood was middle-class and uneventful. By his own admission he was not an outstanding scholar. Loner he may have been, but he showed no special interest in the traditional pursuits of loners. No long hours with his nose buried in books. No solitary Saturday afternoons immersed in the adventures of John Wayne at the neighbourhood cinema.

'I didn't spend much time at the movies,' he told an interviewer. 'I'm not a scholar of Bogart's mannerisms, so I miss a lot of the film references that people like Spielberg and Lucas toss around.'

There were few games of 'dress up and make believe' in Ford's childhood. In fact, the idea of acting didn't occur to him until much later on.

'There is circus in my family, though. My grandfather was a Vaudevillian. My father was briefly a radio actor, became an advertising executive and still does voiceovers for commercials.'

Harrison Ford was educated at Ripon College in North Wisconsin. He spent the best part of three years studying English and Philosophy. 'It was my senior year and suddenly I discovered that I had no idea how I was going to make a living in those two areas, so I just stopped going to classes – they kicked me out a few days before graduation.' Three days before graduation to be precise. 'Bounced in academic disgrace, much to the embarrassment of my parents, who had made a reservation at a motel in town for the ceremony.'

Ejected from the protected existence of college life, Ford found himself face to face with the real world. He married his college sweetheart Mary that summer, despite the fact that he had no job and no prospects. However, he had been involved in a couple of college theatre productions. It seemed natural that he should put this experience to good use.

'I did one season of Summer Stock (the American equivalent of Repertory) immediately after college, in Williams Bay. That's a resort community on the shores of Lake Geneva. Not the Swiss one, the one in Wisconsin. I decided to stick to acting, with drawing room comedy in mind.'

But for some reason, the live stage didn't have what it takes to hold on to Ford. He took the decision to head West. 'I went to Los Angeles,' he recalls. 'I didn't know any of the names of the motion picture studios. I didn't know any actors. I didn't know anything! And of course I'm not Angeleno by birth or by heart – it's just the place where I find myself today. But Los Angeles is where you have to be if you want to be an actor. You have no choice. You go there or New York. I flipped a coin about it. It came up New York, so I flipped again. When you're starting out to be an actor, who wants to go where it's cold and miserable and be poor there? Better to be poor in the sunshine than in the snow. That was my idea, anyway. So we loaded all our stuff into the Volkswagen, drove off and didn't stop until we saw the Pacific. As far as I was concerned, that Ocean must mean California – fine! Let's stop here. Laguna Beach. About 60 miles south of LA. I did a play, *John Brown's Body* at the playhouse there, but the thought of doing it over and over again just stopped me. Luckily, Columbia Pictures' New Talent programme scout saw me and sent me to see the head of casting there.'

Even in 1963 the major Hollywood studios were keeping scores of young good-looking hopefuls on the payroll and used them in bit parts in movies. Ford tells the story of how he was hired and makes it sound like something out of a 1930s musical.

'I walked into this small, heated, walnut-panelled office. There was a little, bald-headed guy with a stub of a cigar, white on white shirt, white on white tie, sitting behind a desk. Two telephones. Behind him a man who looked like a racetrack tout on two more

OPPOSITE: A young Harrison Ford, under contract to Columbia Pictures. '$150 a week and all the respect that implies.' (Columbia Pictures).

phones. I sat in the only chair available, right in front of the desk, and listened to them discussing big names and big money. Then the bald guy looked at me as if he'd discovered a snake in his soup. "Who sent you here?" I told him. He turned to the other guy and said, "Who's that?" "I dunno," the other guy said.

'The bald guy turned back to me. "That's all right...doesn't matter. What's your name? How tall? How much do you weigh? Any special hobbies, talents, capacities? Speak any foreign languages? Okay, fine. If we find anything for you, we'll let you know."

'I walked out of the office, down the hall and pressed the button for the elevator. When it didn't come immediately, I realised that I had to pee. I went round the corner to the bathroom, went in, took a pee, came out and the assistant guy was running down the hall yelling, "Come back, come back." Obviously, if I'd gone down in the elevator, it wouldn't have been worth his while chasing me.

'So I went back to the office. The little bald guy says, "You're not the type we're usually interested in, but how'd'ya like to be under contract?" Sure, absolutely. And about six months later, I was. For $150 a week. And all the respect that implies.'

It might seem to some that Harrison Ford's acting career was well and truly on its way. Perhaps Ford

himself thought that at first, too. But it wasn't going to be that easy.

'That was 1964,' he says, 'and Columbia was still playing 1924. You had to come to the studio every day, in a jacket and a tie, go to acting class, eat in the executive dining room, submit yourself to photo layouts. Six starlets and six fellas playing football on Malibu Beach in front of a Chevrolet Nova for *Argosy* magazine...you know the kind of thing, "Photos courtesy of Columbia Pictures." Horrible, really. Worse than any factory. Nobody ever knew your name at the Studio, or cared a damn about you. I went nuts.'

Nevertheless, Ford stuck it out. 'It was less sophisticated than modelling, but it was a way of being acknowledged as an actor while I learned to act.' At least, that was the plan. But if the truth be known, Ford's career was on 'hold'.

'I wasn't learning anything. But around that time I bought a house near the Hollywood Bowl and decided to take out everything I didn't like about it. I'd never done any carpentry before, but I got the books from the library, got the tools and did it.'

THE MAIDEN VOYAGE

Whatever their other faults in the handling of their contract players, Columbia did sooner or later use the better ones in bit parts in their movies. Eventually, Ford's number came up. He had a part. 'I played a bell boy in *Dead Heat on a Merry-Go-Round* (1966). One day's work. Nothing uplifting. I had to say, "Paging Mr Jones, paging Mr Jones," or something like that and then James Coburn would wave me over and I'd give him a telegram. That was it!'

But Ford's first movie appearance didn't set the film community alight. In fact, his bosses were less than pleased with his 'performance'.

'The guy who was the vice-president of Columbia at the time – maybe I'm spilling the beans here, but that guy is no longer in the business and I am – he called me into his office after that film. Now, remember. All I had to do was deliver a telegram, right?

'"Kid," he says – they always called me "Kid", probably because they didn't know who the hell I was – "Kid, siddown. Lemme tell you a story. First time Tony Curtis ever appeared in a movie, he delivered a bag of groceries. A bag of groceries! You took one look at that person and you knew he was a star. You ain't got it kid! Get back to class, because you ain't going to work again in this studio for six months, maybe a year. Get yourself together!"'

Ford was amazed. 'I thought I had to act like a bellboy...it didn't occur to me till years later that what they wanted me to do was act like a movie star.'

It was as if Ford's hopes for an acting career had been dashed. He was trapped in a seven-year contract with a studio which wouldn't let him act. But eventually he did act again. 'I got a small part in *Luv*(1967),'commented Ford. Small is right. Having trouble remembering what Ford had to do in that one, I checked the cast and credits of the movie meticulously. Ford was so far down the cast list that he must have dropped off the bottom. No mention is made of him in the studio's list of actors for that movie.

BELOW: *Harrison Ford circa 1966. He was twenty-four but looked seventeen. (Columbia Pictures).*

That same year, Columbia Pictures took over production of a Roger Corman movie called *The Long Ride Home* (1967, aka *A Time For Killing*). The movie pitted Glenn Ford's Union soldier Major Walcott against imprisoned Confederate officer Captain Bentley (George Hamilton) in a fairly unremarkable American Civil War drama. Harrison J. Ford turned up in this one playing a young officer, Lieutenant Shaffer. He didn't make very much impression in this one either.

'Was I demoralised?' asks Ford. 'You bet I was. Particularly as the studio thought it would be a good idea if I wore my hair like Elvis Presley and changed my name. I suggested Kurt Affair. After that, there was no more talk of changing names. Not that it would have mattered what I was called. I was going nowhere fast. This was the atmosphere when they let me go.'

It was time for Ford to be called into the headmaster's office and be given another dressing down. 'The head of the studio, Mike Frankovitch, was in Europe, so this other guy had to make the determination whether or not they should take up the option on my contract after eighteen months.

'"Kid," he said – what else? – "as soon as Frankovitch is back I'm going to tell him we ought to get rid of you. I don't think you're worth a thing to us. But I know your wife is pregnant, you need the money, so I'll give you another couple of weeks. Just sign the piece of paper my secretary has. Okay, boy? Now, get out of here!"'

Ford had had enough. He was tired of being pushed around by men behind desks. He told the guy where he could stick his money and was fired on the spot.

'I had that kind of spirit, but nothing behind it. Three days later, I was under contract to Universal.'

OUT OF THE FRYING PAN?

It might seem strange that Harrison Ford would give up one studio situation, which he hated, for another which probably wouldn't be a lot better. In reality there was an improvement, if only a marginal one.

'The situation at Universal was somewhat better. But they never really had the guts to use me outside of television.'

But in among the contract player appearances in such Universal TV shows as *The Virginian*, *The F.B.I.*, *Gunsmoke* (including the episodes *The Sodbusters* and *Wheelan's Men*) and *Ironside*, Ford was assigned to a role in the 1968 Universal movie, *Journey to Shiloh*, another Civil War drama. Ford plays Willie Bill Bearden, one of seven young Texans who leave home under the leadership of Buck Burnett (James Caan) in search of adventure in the Confederate Army. They plan to join up with General Hood's Richmond Raiders but after several adventures en route – one of their number is killed in a card game, they witness the lynching of a runaway slave, Buck falls in love with a saloon girl, Gabrielle (Brenda Scott) – they are inducted into a Pensacola unit because of their outstanding horsemanship. Suddenly, they are face to face with the true horror of war at Shiloh. The Confederates are routed and four

of the youngsters, including Willie Bill, are killed. The survivors of the battle are put to flight and Buck is wounded escaping from the Confederate military police, who are hunting down deserters from Shiloh. Buck regains consciousness in a military hospital, but is horrified to find his arm has been amputated. He learns that the last member of his band, Miller Nalls (Michael Sarrazin), was to be shot as a deserter, but has escaped and is hiding out in a barn severely wounded. Buck defies orders to go to Miller, but finds him close to death. Touched by the story of the seven young men, General Bragg (John Doucette) calls off the military police and allows Buck, the sole survivor, to make his way home.

Ford's role in the film was so minor that it has proved impossible to track down a review that singles out his performance, though the *Monthly Film Bulletin* said of the film in general, 'the acting is often strident and the script too naively emotional not to fall into mawkishness at times…(but) well worth a look.'

Then, abruptly, it seemed that Harrison Ford's luck had taken a turn for the better. He was loaned out by Universal for a role in Michelangelo Antonioni's movie *Zabriskie Point* (1969). Antonioni had made something of a name for himself as a director whose films reached the lucrative 'now' generation. His earlier film *Blowup* had opened to the bafflement of the establishment critics and the delight of the target audiences.

Zabriskie Point tells the story of a rebellious American student, Mark (Mark Frechette) who finds himself involved in a campus riot. When a policeman is shot Mark is a suspect and is forced to lie low. He steals a small private plane and sets off across the Arizona desert, heading nowhere in particular. He crosses paths with Daria (Daria Halprin) who is heading towards Phoenix in a borrowed car for a meeting with her new employer, Lee Allen (Rod Taylor). Mark lands his plane and is given a lift by Daria. They stop in Death Valley and make love amidst the sand dunes. When Daria is stopped by a police patrol, Mark decides that the only way out of his dilemma is to return to the plane and give himself up to the police. He paints the plane with slogans and outlandish colours and sets off for Los Angeles. But when he arrives, a police reception committee is waiting and Mark is shot dead before he can explain. Daria hears the news on the car radio before she arrives at her meeting and for a while seems to deliberate whether or not to continue. Reaching a decision, Daria presses on to Allen's luxurious mountainside villa and, after wandering aimlessly around the house for a while, climbs back into her car and drives some distance from the house. She looks back to the villa and imagines it and all it represents being blasted to smithereens by a huge explosion. Smiling, she continues on her journey to nowhere.

As it turned out, Antonioni seemed to experience inordinate difficulties in achieving the results he wanted with *Zabriskie Point*. The script sported the names of five writers and the movie was recut by the director several times. In the cutting and re-cutting Harrison Ford's part ('In fact, the whole sub-plot,' says Ford) was snipped out and consigned to the oblivion of the cutting room floor. Which is probably just as well. *Zabriskie Point* was not a success and did nothing to enhance the careers of any involved with it.

THE HARRISON FORD STORY

OPPOSITE: Harrison Ford's first film role . . . as a bellboy in Dead Heat on a Merry-Go-Round. *(Columbia Pictures).*

But Universal hadn't given up. They seemed determined to launch Ford in some kind – any kind – of youth orientated film. Their next step was to loan Ford back to Columbia Pictures for the film, *Getting Straight* (1970). The film followed the misadventures of Harry Bailey (Elliott Gould) and his girlfriend Jan (Candice Bergen) as they fought to keep their heads above water on an American University campus beset with student unrest. Eagle-eyed film fans might have spotted Ford in the role of Jake, but the movie was locked in time as a product of the late Sixties and did nothing to open up Ford's career. Though he was growing older and gaining more experience, the parts he was getting were becoming 'smaller and more one-dimensional.

'I was given tiny spaces to fill,' says Ford. 'Nothing where you could take space. Maybe they were right. I probably wasn't ready. But I was getting older. Except, when I was twenty-one every one thought I was seventeen. All soft and putty-like but aging fast on the inside, going crazy. I had to get away from it. Yet I had invested maybe four years and I didn't want to give up. I still wanted to be an actor when I grew up. When I started acting, I thought of it as being an awesome task, exciting and frightening and a wonderful way for someone with no degree to live. I suppose being the son of a former radio actor and advertising executive in charge of Chicago's TV commercials, I should have known better. I was not prepared for the disillusionment I found as an actor in the studio system.'

There was another danger, too. If an actor's face becomes too familiar, then often the studio simply stops using them. 'I was worried that I'd become over-exposed,' says Ford. 'Used up in three seasons and never have a long-term career. So I decided to stop taking small TV parts and become a carpenter. I'd had no training in carpentry, any more than I'd had in acting. But I set my mind to it. My first assignment was a $100,000 recording studio for Sergio Mendes. Fortunately, the Encino Public Library was only three blocks away. I'd be standing on Mendes' roof with a text book in my hand.'

For all Ford's inexperience in carpentry, the business paid well. He made more from that Mendes job than he had for his first walk-on part as the bell-boy in the Coburn picture. Soon, the carpentry game was paying Ford well enough that he could take on his own architects and builders. 'That's when I realised the correlation between money and respect.

Take a lot of money off people and they'll treat you with respect. They'd ask, "How much is all this going to cost me?" And I'd say, "Well I don't know. All I can tell you is that when it's done, it'll be done right."'

At last, Ford was not at the beck and call of the studio heavies. And he was loving every minute of it.

'When I started carpentry,' he recalls, 'I liked it so much partly because it was such a relief from what I'd been doing before. For about eight years in the late Sixties and early Seventies, I did cabinets, furniture, remodelling. It was great! I could see my accomplishments. So I decided not to do any more acting unless the job had a clear career advantage. Altogether, I'd have to say I spent fifteen years in the acting business, but I made my living as a carpenter. I am not a Hollywood success story. Still, I didn't worry about money. I had an understanding wife. I was playing pretty fast and loose with life.'

He had lived like that a few years earlier for a while. That resulted in the famous scar, beneath his lower lip. He picked up that distinguishing feature in a 'fast car crash. I was driving through Laguna Canyon. I had come from my job as an assistant buyer in the knick-knacks and oil paintings department of Bullocks department store and as I turned round to put my seat belt on, I ran into a telegraph pole…later on I ran into a bad stitcher!'

BACK TO ACTING

'When my wife, Mary, became pregnant with our second child, Willard, I realised my health insurance, that I'd had when Ben was born, allowing us to have a baby for about 25 cents a pound, was no longer in force. Because I hadn't made $1,200 in the previous year. So I had to make $1,200 to keep my health insurance. I said, "Well, I've got to do something." And a friend of mine, Fred Roos, was casting a George Lucas picture and said I ought to be in it because it was going to be a big hit. It *was* in every way.'

So Harrison Ford was on his way. But whatever happened to the guys who had given him such a hard time at Columbia? 'Oh, they're still around, but they don't call me "kid" any more. But they still call me. Because they don't care what I think of them, and they don't care what they used to think of me. They don't 'relate' to that. They relate only – totally – to the success of films like *Star Wars*.'

CHAPTER 2

HARRISON FORD:
BREAKING IN

From Touch 'n' Go to Turning Point

'Acting is basically like carpentry – if you
know your craft, you can figure out the logic of
a particular job and submit yourself to it. It all
comes down to detail.'

Harrison Ford

In early 1972, unbeknown to Harrison Ford, a young film-maker called George Lucas was struggling with the Hollywood system to get a pet project off the ground. The movie he wanted to make was a kind of musical autobiography, Fifties/Sixties teenagers wasting away their lives, cruising the streets of small-town California, to the accompaniment of the local radio station blaring out the rock 'n' roll hits of the day.

Lucas had had a qualified success with his first feature film, *THX 1138*, made for Warner Brothers. That is, critics had spoken highly of the film, but the public stayed away in droves. Needless to say, Warners were not interested in financing what they viewed as an indulgent, un-commercial project, despite the very commercial title of *American Graffiti*.

Lucas had no choice but to hawk the project around the other movie factories in town. He hired former film school class mates Willard Huyck and Gloria Katz to help him develop a 'treatment', an outline of the story, in an effort to give the movie moguls something they could understand. All went well. United Artists gave the go-ahead, and a sum of money, for Lucas to produce a full script. Lucas contacted Huyck and Katz to ask them to write the screenplay. However, they had just landed a deal to write and direct their own horror picture in Britain, and couldn't find time to help Lucas with the script. (For the record, the horror movie became the undistinguished *Messiah of Evil*, 1972.)

Lucas was in a bind. He asked his *Graffiti* line producer, Gary Kurtz, to find a substitute writer. Kurtz suggested another film school peer, Richard Walters. Lucas, sure that his project was in safe hands, set off for the Cannes Film Festival where *THX 1138* was entered in the competition.

When Lucas returned from France, he read the Walters script and wasn't pleased with what he found. Walters had done a good job, all right, but it wasn't the story Lucas had in mind. To make matters worse, Kurtz had spent all the United Artists advance on this one screenplay.

Luckily for Lucas, Huyck and Katz returned from their horror movie expedition to Britain, and agreed to pitch in and help out.

Despite United Artists dropping out of the project, all went well. Lucas managed to interest Universal. A young executive there was very keen to give young film-makers the opportunity (and a very low budget) to make the kind of films they wanted too. This executive, Ned Tannen, gave Lucas $750,000 to make the picture, provided Lucas's old friend and mentor, Francis Coppola, flush from his *Godfather* success, agreed to become producer.

With the go-ahead from Universal, Lucas engaged Coppola man Fred Roos to cast the film. Roos and Lucas conducted an old-time Hollywood talent search in an effort to find just the right performers for the roles, each of which portrayed (perhaps a little indulgently) a different facet of Lucas's own personality. Finally, Lucas selected four or five actors for each of the principal roles and conducted screen tests using video equipment, an unheard of procedure in Hollywood at the time. The idea was to assemble a cast that worked well as a group rather than relying on a band of actors who were individually outstanding. Strangely enough, the final selection each turned out to have star careers ahead of them: Ron Howard (who went from the phenomenal success of TV's *Happy Days* to directing his own feature films). Richard Dreyfuss (star roles in *Jaws*, *Close Encounters of the Third Kind* and an Oscar for *The Goodbye Girl*), Candy Clark, Cindy Williams and Kathleen Quinlan. And helping out in the secondary parts were Suzanne Somers, Bo Hopkins, Paul Le Mat and...Harrison Ford.

'I was Bob Falfa – the boy in the cowboy hat,' Ford later remarked.

In fact, Fred Roos was the only real friend Ford had made during his days at the Columbia sweat-shop. Roos remembered Ford and suggested him to Lucas for the part of Falfa.

But Ford attributed his success at landing the role to a basic change in attitude about the acting business. He had been earning his living as a successful businessman for a couple of years, and didn't rely on the *Graffiti* part for his livelihood. 'When I went for the interview, I wasn't there as a person who needed a job to put bread on the table,' says Ford. 'I had, for once, a real life behind me. When you're an out-of-work actor and you walk into an audition, you're an empty vessel. So this was a significant change in my personality. I had got my pride back.'

It must have been that forthright confident air that made Lucas pick Ford for the Falfa role. In the film, Falfa is a cocky out-of-towner who roars in in a black hot-rod to take on the resident champion in a drag race. Each time he is seen in the film he is with a different girl, eventually carrying Ron Howard's girlfriend Laurie (Cindy Williams), with him during the final drag race of the picture.

The shooting schedule for *American Graffiti* was gruelling. The night-time location filming began at nine in the evening and broke, just before dawn at around five-thirty.

'It was fun,' smiles Harrison Ford, 'It was like a party, but not a Hollywood party. It was a real low-budget movie, even for those days. I only got a couple of hundred dollars a week. There were no dressing rooms. The actors sat in the same trailer as the costumes.'

Ford was the oldest of the principal players on the film, though rather than setting an example of professional sobriety, he was more often than not the mastermind behind many of the pranks played on unfortunate victims during the filming.

At the 'wrap' party, at the end of filming, Lucas screened a twenty-minute extract for the cast and crew. Most were sure that they were on to something good. When the lights went up, Ford turned to his neighbour, Cindy Williams, and said, 'This is great!'

The film had been shot, on schedule, inside 28 working days (or, rather, nights), but George Lucas's problems were far from over. Universal didn't like the movie and wanted to re-cut it. It was here that Coppola decided to earn his money as producer. He flatly refused to allow Universal to tamper with the film, and offered Ned Tanner a cheque for the whole of the budget, in effect, buying *American Graffiti*, lock, stock and soundtrack, from Universal. After much arguing back and forth, Tanner got his way and made a couple of cuts, then previewed the film. *American Graffiti* was a hit with everyone except Harrison Ford and Richard Dreyfuss, who sneaked out of the preview before the film ended, because they were so embarrassed at their big-screen debut.

Graffiti was released and eventually pulled in a staggering $117 million on the modest outlay of $750,000. Universal made its money back 50-fold!

The scenes that disappeared were Terry the Toad's encounter with the fast-talking car salesman, John Milner and Carol's walk through the automobile scrapyard and Bob Falfa singing *Some Enchanted Evening* to Laurie. Ford's scene was cut, not because his singing was inferior (though, admittedly, it's not Caruso either!) but because Rodgers and Hammerstein's estates, who owned copyright on the song, wanted too much money for its inclusion in the movie.

However, for the 1978 re-release, these scenes were reinstated.

WHO WAS THAT MASKED CASTING DIRECTOR?

It was Fred Roos, again, who was responsible for getting Harrison Ford his next two roles. Francis Coppola was putting together another project, the highly praised *The Conversation*. Naturally he hired Fred Roos to cast the movie. And, inevitably, Roos turned once again to Harrison Ford for one of the smaller, but hardly less vital, parts in the picture.

'I still did the odd carpentry job after *American Graffiti*,' recalls Ford. 'But before too long there was

Coppola's film, *The Conversation*, which I did with Hackman. I turned up playing an evil young henchman (Martin Stett, who works for Robert Duvall's Director character) in that movie. There was no role there until I decided to make him a homosexual.'

The Conversation tells the story of surveillance expert Harry Caul (Gene Hackman), who records a conversation between a young couple as they walk through San Francisco. When Harry plays the tape back in his workshop, he notices a sentence in the conversation which suggests the couple are in some kind of danger. He takes the tape to the Director (Robert Duvall) of the large corporation which hired him, but on an impulse refuses to hand the tapes over to the Director's assistant, Martin Stett (Harrison Ford). Later, while visiting a surveillance equipment exhibition, Harry runs into Stett again. The young man tries to put pressure on Harry to hand over the tapes. Harry refuses. At the same exhibition, he meets and befriends another investigator, Bernie Moran (Allen Garfield). They have a few drinks together and return to Harry's workshop for a party. Also at the party is a call-girl, Meredith (Elizabeth MacRae) with whom Harry spends some time. But when he wakes up, Harry finds that the tapes of the conversation have been stolen. He tries to contact the Director but fails. Fearing that a murder is about to be committed, he takes a room next to the one in which the young couple have arranged to meet. He

BELOW: *As the hot-rodder Bob Falfa in George Lucas's* American Graffiti *(1973). Every time you see Falfa in the movie, he's with a different girl.* (Lucasfilm Ltd).

breaks into the couple's room and is horrified to find that a murder *has* been committed. The Director has been killed, apparently by the couple that Harry thought were in danger. Back at his apartment, Harry is warned to keep what he knows to himself as he, too, is under surveillance. Harry searches his own apartment thoroughly for the listening device but finds nothing.

The Conversation received much praise from the critics. *Monthly Film Bulletin's* David Wilson said, 'The *Conversation* is an unqualified success, a complex, reverberating study of a man trapped by guilt...It is a measure of that success...that the comparison which most obviously suggests itself, *Blow-Up*, leaves Antonioni's film looking empty and inert.'

But good though Ford's performance in *The Conversation* might have been, again he went unnoticed by the critics. The one big success still eluded him.

Ford next had a walk-on part in the TV-movie *The Trial of Lt Calley* ('I played the witness who cries,' says Ford) and a more substantial role as the eldest son of Sarah Miles's Jennifer Blackwood in the lavish TV production of James Michener's novel *Dynasty*.

Dynasty is a sprawling tale of the fortunes of the Blackwood family and their migration to Westmore, Ohio in 1823. John Blackwood (Harris Yulin), the head of the family is a man of unbending principles whose dearest ambition it is to farm the 100 acre piece of land he has acquired. His wife, Jennifer (Sarah Miles) and his brother Matt (Stacy Keach) both feel there is more money to be made in the carriage business. Eventually, Jennifer leaves John for Matt after being accused of infidelity by her husband. But the relationship doesn't work out and Jennifer

returns to John. Realising the depth of her husband's hatred for her she endeavours to build the Blackwood carriage business into an empire. Matt returns to Westmore and tries to convince John to sell the farmland to the railroad for a huge profit. Though John refuses, Jennifer's youngest son, Carver (Gerrit Graham) conspires with Matt to kill John and sell the land. After John's death, Jennifer, unaware of the conspiracy, passes over her eldest son, Mark (Harrison Ford) and appoints Matt to run the Blackwood business.

Variety complained that Dynasty's 'last half hour concentrates too much on Miles's ungrateful grown-up offspring' and that it 'really encompassed too wide a time span to be handled properly in a two-hour movie.'

Harrison Ford was still an acting carpenter.

But by this time, the *American Graffiti* director George Lucas had finalised a deal with Twentieth Century-Fox to make a space adventure movie called *Star Wars*. Ford was familiar with the project, but nurtured no ambitions about being in the movie. After all, he hadn't been one of the principle players in *Graffiti* and probably felt his contribution had been minimal.

'George (Lucas) had let it be known that he wasn't going to use anybody from *American Graffiti*,' says Ford. 'Not because we'd disappointed him, but he was writing a whole new thing and needed new faces. But old Fred Roos did it again. He prevailed on George to see me after he'd seen everyone else.'

The story of how Harrison Ford ended up with the role of Han Solo is another one of those tales that Ford tells better than anyone else. He recounted it within a short interview for the London events magazine, *Time Out*.

OPPOSITE: *In* The Trial of Lt Calley. (*Universal*). ABOVE: *As the nasty Martin Stett, assistant to* The Director *in Coppola's* The Conversation (1974). (*Paramount*).

'The reason I ran into George Lucas again was because Francis Coppola's art director inveigled me into installing a very elaborate raised panel in his studio office. Now, I knew they were casting and I thought it a bit coy to be around Francis's office, being a carpenter, during the day. So I did the work at night. Well, one day something came up and I got stuck and I had to work at the studios during the day. And, sure enough, that was the day that George Lucas was doing the casting for *Star Wars*.

'There I was, on my knees in the doorway, and in comes Francis Coppola, George Lucas, four other captains of the industry and Richard Dreyfuss. In fact, Dreyfuss came through first and made a big joke out of being my assistant. That made me feel just great. I felt about the size of a pea after they walked through. But, weeks later, when they'd tested everybody else in the world, I got the part.'

Ford is guilty of a little over-simplification here. The casting for *Star Wars* was as meticulous, at the very least, as the casting on *American Graffiti*. Lucas knew he was going to have to interview literally hundreds of young actors and young hopefuls just to find the three people to portray the key lead roles. He joined forces with another young director making his first major picture, Brian De Palma, who was looking for a teenage cast for *Carrie*. For about eight weeks, De Palma and Lucas were seeing 30-40 young actors and actresses a day. Lucas sat quietly making notes and entering the names of those who particularly impressed him on a Second Interview list. After Lucas tripped over Ford in the doorway of Coppola's office, the young film-maker approached Ford for assistance with the video tests for the *Star Wars* auditions. The idea was that Ford, whom Lucas felt at ease with, would read the male parts for the actresses testing for the role of Princess Leia. Ford didn't mind doing the favour for Lucas, whom he liked, but after a time became irritated with having to read a part which he thought he would never play. According to Dale Pollock's book, *Skywalking*, it was Ford's churlishness that won him the part of Han Solo. It's far more likely that George Lucas saw in Harrison Ford elements of the character he envisaged for Solo. Ford had a certain forthright and honest way of expressing himself that isn't a million light years away from Solo's lines in the movie.

At one stage, Lucas was considering a black actor for the role of Solo. This idea probably evolved into the character of Lando Calrissian in *The Empire Strikes Back*.

But also to be taken into consideration, was Lucas's unique concept of ensemble casting. Lucas had decided on Harrison Ford, Mark Hamill and Carrie Fisher as one trio. But if any of them had been unable to take part in the film, Lucas had a reserve team waiting in the wings to step in. It was all of one group or all of the other – no mixing and matching. Lucas's second group was Christopher Walken, Will Selzer and ex-Penthouse Pet Terri Nunn.

'And for me, at least,' says Ford, 'it was obvious what the relationship would be, simply by looking at the others. It was apparent the characters were very contemporary and the situation very simple – without meaning that in a derogatory way. It was simply straightforward, a clear human story. I mean I didn't have to act science fiction.'

George Lucas had worked out backgrounds for all his characters. Solo had been abandoned by space gypsies at a very early age and was raised by creatures called Wookies until he was twelve. He eventually became a cadet at the Space Academy, but was thrown out for selling exam papers to his peers. Eventually he became a smuggler, living outside the laws of the Empire. Yet at the same time, Lucas knew that his actors could add the little touches that would bring the characters to life on the screen.

'Very little time was wasted,' says Ford in the Lucas biography, *Skywalking*. 'George didn't have an authoritarian attitude like so many directors: "Kid, I've been in this business twenty-five years. Trust me." He was different. He knew the movie was based so strongly on the relationship between the three of us, he encouraged our contributions.'

It's the little contributions Ford makes to the characters he's playing that makes him such an interesting actor. Which shows that Lucas's shrewdness won out over his own 'all new faces' rule for *Star Wars*. Ford goes on to explain how he went about filling in the spaces in Solo's personality.

'George Lucas gave me a lot of freedom to change little parts of the dialogue which weren't comfortable.' Ford is being charitable here. In *Skywalking* it says that Ford's favourite way of pulling Lucas's leg during filming was to say, 'You can type this shit, George, but you sure can't say it.'

'We worked together on it,' continues Ford. 'I really like working with him.'

The part of Han Solo was the biggest chance of Ford's career to show what he could do as an actor. 'This was the first time I had a character big enough to

BELOW: *The principal players of Star Wars (1977). Mark Hamill, Carrie Fisher, Peter Mayhew and Harrison Ford. (Lucasfilm Ltd).*

take space instead of just filling in spaces as I did at Columbia and Universal. I could do that for the first time.'

Ford had worked with big name, heavyweight actors before, but never with such a 'legend' as Sir Alec Guinness. Most of the cast were in awe of Sir Alec and Ford was no exception.

'He gave me many sleepless nights. I'd be thinking, "I'm supposed to be in a movie with Sir Alec Guinness. He'll laugh at me just once…and I'll pack up and go home." But, of course, he never did. He's really a very kind and generous person.'

When questioned by *Ritz* magazine whether Ford was using the title 'Sir Alec' out of respect or because Guinness insisted on it, he replied with his customary tact, 'Let's just say he prefers it.'

A NEW HOPE

Though *Star Wars* was Ford's first major role in a major movie, the character wasn't really the star of the show. Solo stood closer to Stage Right, while the essence of the tale pivoted around the character of Luke Skywalker (Mark Hamill).

'A Long Time Ago, in a Galaxy Far, Far Away…' An Evil Emperor, with the aid of an equally evil Lord Darth Vader (David Prowse, voice by James Earl Jones), rules the Galaxy with an iron fist in steel gauntlet. Understandably, not everyone is happy with this arrangement and a rebel movement, led by Princess Leia Organa (Carrie Fisher), is conducting a hit-and-run, terrorist-style campaign against the oppressive Imperial Forces. The adventure begins when Princess Leia's ship, on its way to the rebel outpost at Alderaan with the stolen plans for the Empire's 'Death Star' space station, is captured by the forces of Darth Vader. Leia hides the plans inside a diminutive robot, R2-D2 (Kenny Baker), and sends him, and his golden robot companion C-3PO (Anthony Daniels), to the planet Tatooine to seek out the former Jedi warrior, Obi-wan Kenobi (Sir Alec Guinness).

The robots fall into the hands of Owen Lars (Phil Brown) a farmer of the region. Owen's nephew, Luke Skywalker (Mark Hamill), accidently discovers the message concealed in the small robot and soon finds himself, along with the two robots, at the home of the warrior Obi-wan discussing how best to get the vital plans to the Rebel Alliance on Alderaan. Obi-wan reveals that Luke's father was also a Jedi Knight and that Luke must learn the secrets of the Jedi if he is to see the plans safely into the Rebels' hands.

Luke returns to his Uncle Owen's farm to explain his plans, but is horrified to find that the Imperial Forces have been there before him and killed both Owen and Aunt Beru (Shelagh Fraser). Luke swears revenge against the Empire and sets off with Obi-wan and the two robots for the space port of Mos Eisley, in the hope of hitching a ride to Alderaan on a space freighter.

Obi-wan meets up with a pair of freelance space adventurers, Han Solo (Harrison Ford) and his First Mate Chewbacca the Wookie (Peter Mayhew) and strikes a bargain for their passage to the rebel base.

Meanwhile, aboard the Death Star, Princess Leia is being interrogated by Grand Moff Tarkin (Peter Cushing) and Darth Vader. Receiving no satisfactory reply to his questions, Tarkin gives the order for the destruction of Alderaan.

Back aboard Solo's ship, the Millennium Falcon, Obi-wan, through his mastery of The Force, 'feels' the destruction of the planet telepathically. The Falcon emerges from hyper-space where Alderaan should be to discover only a meteor shower and, in the distance, a 'small moon' which has no business being there. Solo noses forward to investigate but the ship is gripped in a powerful tractor beam and drawn aboard the 'moon' – in reality the Death Star.

Our heroes manage to elude the Imperial search parties put aboard the Falcon by Vader, but discover the Princess is being held captive elsewhere on the station. They decide to split up. Obi-wan is to neutralise the tractor beam holding the Falcon and Luke, Han and Chewie, hindered rather than helped by the droids, will attempt to rescue the Princess.

The rescue team reaches the prison block but an altercation with the guards alerts the Imperial troops to their presence. Solo tries to convince a curious officer who calls the prison block on the intercom that nothing is amiss and, failing, blasts the communications console to bits with the dour comment, 'Boring conversation anyway!' They succeed in rescuing the Princess from her cell and make their way back to the Falcon via the Death Star's garbage disposal system.

In the meantime, Obi-wan has succeeded in putting the tractor beam out of action and is on his way back to the ship. Unfortunately, he runs into Darth Vader on the way and engages the villain in

BELOW: *Chewbacca (Peter Mayhew) and Han Solo (Harrison Ford) flee from the Imperial Stormtroopers along the corridors of the Death Star. (Lucasfilm Ltd).*

hand-to-hand combat to allow the others to escape. Luke is dumbstruck to see his mentor deliberately let Vader strike him down in order to allow them to escape.

Our heroes reach the nearest Rebel outpost with the Death Star in close pursuit and mobilise the rebel fighter squadrons for an all-out assault on the battle station. The idea is that a small explosive charge, lobbed into a certain exhaust port, will bring about a chain reaction which will utterly destroy the Death Star and cause a serious set-back to the Emperor and his forces. It is Luke, with some last minute help from Han Solo, who delivers the fatal shot. Then, back at the Rebel base, Luke, Han and Chewbacca are cheered by the massed armies of the Rebel Alliance and are rewarded by Princess Leia in a rousing Happy Ending.

THE CHANGING FACE OF THE MOVIES

When *Star Wars* opened in the United States on May 25th, 1977, it garnered rave reviews and within months had become the most successful movie of all time. Several critics likened Ford's performance in the Han Solo role to John Wayne's style of acting.

This was news to Ford, never a movie fan himself.

'I never thought about that,' says Ford, 'until I kept seeing it mentioned in the reviews.' Besides, Ford was well aware that it would be impossible to get away with imitating other actors for very long.

'If I end up acting like John Wayne, and I know I'm acting like John Wayne, then I'm in heaps of trouble. But if I don't realise I'm acting like John Wayne, and I am, then that is simply part of my subconscious supplying something that is necessary for the role. I was never aware of doing a routine. Acting is so intensely personal that if you're not operating – totally – within your own resources, there comes a moment when you'll be stuck, you won't know who to imitate. Much better to use only your own personality and resources as a tool and keep them both sharp and well-oiled.'

Probably Ford's finest moment in *Star Wars* is when he is in the prison block of the Death Star trying to rescue the Princess. Both Solo and Luke are disguised in Imperial Storm Trooper costumes, with Chewbacca posing as their prisoner. The three dispatch the prison guards – noisily – and draw the attention of the officer in charge of the detention area. The officer calls the prison block on the intercom and demands to know what is happening. It's left to Solo

OPPOSITE: *Space Buccaneer: Outlaw Han Solo (Harrison Ford), blaster in hand, strikes a heroic pose before his ship the Millennium Falcon.* BELOW: *Han and the Princess (Carrie Fisher) have the first of their long series of differences in Star Wars. (Lucasfilm Ltd).*

to try to convince the unseen Imperial officer that all is well. Realising that his reassurances are falling on deaf ears, Solo fires his blaster into the control panel to cut off the irritating stream of questions. Solo's sense of desperation is portrayed with nervous realism and, more importantly, with humour. The scene was played that way after careful consideration by Ford, 'and done in one take. I never learned the dialogue for it because I wanted to show desperation. I told George Lucas I wanted to do it all the way through first time. I just said, "Stop me if I'm really bad." He didn't.'

One side effect of the success of *Star Wars* was that it conferred instant celebrity on the three principle players. For an actor who values his privacy, that could have been a problem for Harrison Ford. 'Fortunately, I don't have as unique a physiognomy as Carrie or Mark do, so I'm much less recognised in the streets – about which I'm very happy. That could get heavy. It happens infrequently enough, and people are usually very nice, because the film is very broadly accepted – so that's a pleasure. But when they know where we're going to be, and they're sitting outside the hotel – all these autograph people – sometimes that's a drag. But none of that really bothers me.'

Compounding the fame achieved by Ford through his appearance in *Star Wars* was all the merchandising that trailed in the wake of the movie. Suddenly, the toy shops were full of plastic Han Solo figures, jigsaws bearing Ford's features and assorted paraphernalia. And, in addition to the toys, there was the fact that just about every magazine published was finding excuses to report on the *Star Wars* phenomenon. There were novelisations of the film, comic strip adaptations by juvenile publishing giant *Marvel Comics* and a series of novels, unrelated to the film, starring Han Solo and his Wookie friend Chewbacca. So far, there have been three Han Solo novels, *Han Solo at Stars' End*, *Han Solo and the Lost Legacy* and *Han Solo's Revenge*, all written by Brian Daley and published by Sphere Books.

The other major change in Ford's life brought about by the success of *Star Wars* was the financial one.

'I believe in the work ethic,' says Ford. 'That was the middle class way I was brought up. When I was offered Han Solo, I was paid less for that than when I was a carpenter.'

That was so while he was actually working on the film. But Ford, like Carrie Fisher and Mark Hamill, later received a percentage of the film's profits. Two thirds of a percent may not sound like much, but that fraction of a point totted up a healthy $53,000 for Ford in the first three months that *Star Wars* was on release.

'Not that money means very much in my life. But suddenly having it made it possible to move into a large house in the Hollywood Hills and equip a large workshop on the premises where I now spend all my spare time making furniture. I don't think success has changed me. Sure, I live in a big house. But I still manage to be a pretty private sort of a guy. My greatest pleasure is my work and the nearest thing I've got to a hobby is my carpentry. I don't go to parties and I'm not involved in the Hollywood scene. Who knows, maybe if I had socialised a bit more, success would have come much sooner, because in Hollywood, to succeed, you have to know the right people. By some irony, all the right people – like George Lucas and Francis Coppola – all knew me, and I didn't even have to hustle for their attention.'

And in the months that followed, while Ford was waiting for work to begin on the *Star Wars* sequel, *The Empire Strikes Back*, he didn't have to hustle for the attention of other film makers either. In fact, Ford was the busiest of the *Star Wars* stars during that period.

'That could be because I made an effort to take advantage of the film offers that being in *Star Wars* gave me,' he later said. 'I think people in this industry realise that I've played, and am capable of playing, these different types of characters. I was able to do small parts once in a while due to the popularity of *Star Wars*. I've been really lucky to have *Star Wars* as a part of my life.'

OPPOSITE: *Han Solo (Harrison Ford) battles the dia-noga monster in the Death Star trash compactor for the life of his friend Luke (Mark Hamill). (Lucasfilm Ltd).*

CHAPTER 3

HARRISON FORD: NEW DIRECTIONS

From Star Wars to Wars Star . . .

'When I saw *Star Wars* before it was released, I realised the power of it as a piece of film making, and I set out deliberately to try and find something that would contrast with the character of Han Solo.'

Harrison Ford

The principal photography of *Star Wars* was completed in the August of 1976. It would be nine months before the movie was unleashed on the unsuspecting American public. But Harrison Ford didn't sit around, and wait for success to come to him. The role in *Star Wars* was his biggest achievement in the eleven years he had been in movies. He was aware that Han Solo had been a major role in a major film. If he was to avoid the typecasting he feared would follow in the wake of *Star Wars* he had to make his move immediately. He cast around for a part which would avoid the flippant derring-do of the Solo character, and found it in a middleweight Hollywood movie called *Heroes*.

Heroes was the film which marked the big-screen debut of Henry Winkler. Winkler had shot to fame in the phenominally successful *Happy Days* TV series, a show based, perhaps ironically, certainly unofficially, on *American Graffiti*. Winkler had grown tired of being so irreversibly identified with 'The Fonz' and had selected *Heroes* for his escape from television. The story concerned the uncertain adventures of a returning Vietnam veteran, whose ambition it is to set up a worm farm in nowheresville, California, and his relationships with his best pal (Harrison Ford) and his girl (Sally Field). Jeremy Paul Kagan was the director.

'I did *Heroes* for short money,' says Ford. 'It wasn't a big part, and I wasn't paid big money.'

The filming of *Heroes* was straightforward enough except for one hiccup which involved Harrison Ford and occurred before even a foot of film had run through the cameras.

'Ten days before shooting *Heroes*,' recalls Ford, 'Jeremy changed my character from a mid-Western to a Missouri farm-boy. So off I went to Missouri with a tape-recorder to learn the accent. I bummed around for about three days and went and met the actual type I was going to play – a guy interested in cars. I went into an auto-part store and told them I was a writer, because if you tell them you're an actor, you spend the rest of the time talking about movies – and it also puts a certain distance between you and them.'

When it was released, *Heroes* proved not to be the cinema box-office success Henry Winkler was looking for. The film was over-long and patchy and sank without a trace.

'It was a good part,' says Ford philosophically, 'but Henry Winkler was the real star of the film.'

THE RETURN OF THE ROOS

Harrison Ford's next film role was yet another piece of space filling, which he did at the request of his old friend Fred Roos. Francis Coppola was about to begin work on his latest project, a Vietnam war tale which had been written by John Milius and had originally been slated to be directed by George Lucas and produced only by Coppola. As it worked out, Lucas had stepped aside and Coppola himself ended up in the director's chair. The film was the now legendary *Apocalypse Now*, which was shot in the Phillipines and starred Martin Sheen, Marlon Brando and Robert Duvall.

'Most of my scenes were shared with Martin Sheen,' recalls Ford. 'It wasn't a big role for me, just a nine-day cameo as a US Army Intelligence Colonel. I had my hair cut short and presented another image, Vietnam style.'

As, perhaps, a tip of the director's hat to Lucas's early involvement in the movie, Coppola had Harrison Ford's character wear a name-tag on his uniform which read 'Col G. Lucas'.

'It's just the one scene,' says Ford, 'the laundry list scene – it told the audience all they needed to know for the rest of the movie. And when George (Lucas) saw it, the scene was half-way over before he recognised me. That was exactly the way I wanted it.'

When asked by writer Tony Crawley how he would compare Lucas and Coppola as film-makers, Ford replied 'It's really presumptuous for an actor to get into that kind of discussion. More so for me, I'm not intellectually equipped to make such judgements. Let's see – they both have beards and glasses, and a difference in personality. I know what the differences are, but it would take me about two days to explain it. Certainly, they both allow their actors enormous freedom. Francis lets you make a choice and then moves everything to support you, to make it work for you. He's really delightful.'

But as much as Ford may have enjoyed the experience, brief as it was, on *Apocalypse Now*, it was really only space filling. His next role, as the American Ranger Lieutenant-Colonel Barnsby in *Force Ten From Navarone*, gave him a little more to do.

LEARNING THE WAYS OF THE FORCE

Taking the role in *Force Ten From Navarone* was probably one of the sounder career decisions made by Harrison Ford during the period that immediately followed *Star Wars*. Although it was another supporting role, the fact that it was a major Hollywood style movie made it preferable to a leading role in a small independent production.

'It's fun to do those supporting roles, because they're good character pieces,' Ford pointed out to an interviewer. 'The problem is that they don't usually write character parts as the leads of the movies. Unfortunately, you can't always play the supporting roles because of the complicated vision that people in this industry have. Hollywood only really takes notice when you're being paid the money and given the billing that a 'lead actor' gets. That's why *Force Ten from Navarone* was important for me to do. Its cast was a 'package of big names' which included me.'

Force Ten from Navarone was a belated sequel to the 1961 war adventure *The Guns of Navarone* and tells how the only survivors of the first adventure, Major Mallory (here played by Robert Shaw) and Sergeant Miller (Edward Fox) are sent to Yugoslavia to team up with Lt Col Mike Barnsby (Harrison Ford) and his squad of US Rangers. The object of the exercise is to find and eliminate Nicolai Lescovar, the German spy who sabotaged the original mission and who is now posing as a Yugoslavian resistance fighter. Mallory and Miller hijack an RAF Lancaster – to lessen the chance of betrayal – but are shot down over Yugoslavia, captured by Capt Drazak and handed over to Major Schroeder of the occupying German Army. Mallory concocts a story that he is an escaped prisoner with access to a huge store of penicillin and, with Barnsby, is permitted to set off to retrieve it, accompanied by Schroeder's mistress, Maritza (Barbara Bach). But Maritza is also the daughter of the local partizan chief Major Petrovitch (Alan Badel) and allows them to escape to join the Resistance fighters. When Mallory learns that the Germans are about to mount an offensive using the bridge that Barnsby's men have come to destroy, Maritza engineers the escape of the rest of the Allied soldiers from the hands of the Germans. Miller and Mallory plan to destroy the bridge by exploding a nearby dam. Unfortunately, their supply drop is discovered by the Germans, who bomb the area and kill Maritza into the bargain. Mallory plans a raid on a German supply depot to obtain the necessary explosives and during the operation, the partisan Capt Radicek is revealed to be Lescovar and is shot dead by Barnsby. The dam is blown and the bridge is swept away, but Mallory and his team are trapped behind enemy lines.

Ford is the first to admit that there wasn't very much in *Force Ten from Navarone* he could work on. 'Mike Barnsby was one of those macho, tough-guy parts that everyone *thought* I should be doing.' Yet, in another interview, he did talk about the character as though he respected the kind of person Barnsby was. 'He's a man of real capacity. He flies, he fights, he's got brains, but everything works against him. At the last minute he gets the Robert Shaw and James Fox characters tacked onto his mission, so there's a lot of adversity in the relationship between them, until he begins to need them and they begin to need him – a

nice kind of continuity of cross purposes that become established and finally resolved. An interesting character. I think it'll work.'

When *Force Ten from Navarone* was released it wasn't well received by the critics, though *Playboy's* Bruce Williamson gave the film a cautious thumbs-up, saying, '(Director) Guy Hamilton builds *Force Ten* into a straightforward, man-size adventure – a nostalgic toast to the good old war years, when we unequivocally rooted for our side to win.'

The *Monthly Film Bulletin* was less charitable. 'Leadenly scripted and directed, this rather belated sequel to the *Guns of Navarone* is depressingly short on thrills and almost completely lacking in suspense.'

In the light of the adverse criticism, Ford was given the chance to answer in a post release interview. '*Force Ten from Navarone* was an attempt, in a way, to objectify the success of *Star Wars*. It wasn't a personal success for me. It was George's movie, his success. Nonetheless, I wanted to take advantage of the chance to work. And it was a job I did for the money. And I was lost, because I didn't know what the story was about. I didn't have anything to act. There was no reason for my character being there. I had no part of the story that was important to tell. I had a hard time taking the stage with the bull that I was supposed to be doing. I can't do that, and I won't ever do that again. It wasn't a bad film. There were honest people involved making an honest effort. But it wasn't the right thing for me to do.'

Harrison Ford was then moved from one World

BELOW: *As Mike Barnsby in* Force Ten from Navarone *(1978), a ripping yarn of World War II derring-do. (Columbia).*

War Two tale straight into another. 'After *Force Ten* I was looking forward to doing some building alterations to my house in the Hollywood Hills when Kris Kristofferson dropped out of *Hanover Street* in England,' explains Ford. 'They asked me to come to London and take over his role at very short notice. I played an American B-52 bomber pilot stationed in wartime Britain who falls in love with an English nurse (Lesley-Anne Down) married to a British Intelligence Officer (Christopher Plummer). I enjoyed making it, but the long schedule meant it was quite some time before I saw my home again.'

Despite the fact that Ford got along well with his co-stars, there were other reasons why little is recorded about Ford's involvement in the movie. 'I don't even like to think about *Hanover Street*,' said Ford just before the release of *Raiders of the Lost Ark*. 'The director (Peter Hyams) and I did *not* get along. I've never even seen the film.' All of which begs the question, then why do the film? Ford has an answer for that. 'My motivation for doing *Hanover Street* was because I had never kissed a female human being on the screen before. The characters I played were totally sexless, and here was a movie that was being touted as a romance. That was a clear, obvious reason for doing it.' Then he added, 'There are a lot of other reasons, which may or may not have been the right ones for doing it.'

Said *Playboy*'s Bruce Williamson, 'Ford, as a romantic leading man, is fairly stolid and one-dimensional, labouring hard to simulate the kind of casual charm that Redford, Newman and a dozen other male actors must work hard to conceal when they want to be taken seriously. Hyams gives us a pair of lovers who seldom appear to enjoy each other very much.' Uncharitable, perhaps, but cinema audiences seemed to agree on the whole and the film, although moderately successful, set no box-office records.

GO WEST

It was 1978. Although, unlike Mark Hamill and Carrie Fisher, Harrison Ford had not signed up before *Star Wars* for all three movies, he had agreed to appear in *The Empire Strikes Back*. Ford had negotiated with George Lucas for better terms. He also wanted to see the character of Han Solo become 'more dashing'. Lucas agreed readily to the terms, although, in the end, Ford ended up making no more than his two co-stars from the *Star Wars* sequel.

In the meantime, Ford had just time for one more movie before returning to the camp of George Lucas, *The Frisco Kid*.

The project had originally come up during the filming of *Heroes*. In his interview in *Playboy* for August 1977, Henry Winkler mentioned that he was considering, as his third movie, a project about an immigrant Hasidic rabbi crossing America from East to West to set up a rabbinate in San Francisco. It wasn't made clear which role he was considering, but

it was probably through Winkler that Ford came to be in the movie.

The Frisco Kid is an alleged comedy from the otherwise talented director Robert Aldrich which chronicles the adventures of Polish rabbi, Avram Belinsky, who is one of the poorest students at an orthodox Jewish academy. The older rabbis, more to get rid of Avram than anything else, decide to send him to America to head the Jewish community in Frisco and marry the daughter, Sarah Mindl (Beege Barkett), of the community's most prominent member. Avram arrives in Philadelphia only to find he has missed his connection to San Francisco. Three doubtful looking characters offer to take him overland for $50, but end up by robbing the rabbi and leaving him for dead in the middle of nowhere. He is helped by an Amish community, then continues on his way by train. But the train is held up by an outlaw, Tommy Lillard (Harrison Ford) and Avram ends up working on a railroad gang. With the money he earns,

he buys a horse and sets out again for the West Coast, but disaster strikes again when he loses his horse and is left in the middle of the desert with no food. He is rescued by Tommy who reluctantly agrees to take him to San Francisco. On the way, Tommy takes time out to rob a bank and Avram ends up on the run from the law. He and Tommy are captured by Indians but are accepted by the tribe when Avram demonstrates his courage in his religious faith. Later Avram runs across the three men who robbed him earlier and confronts them, only to be saved at the last moment by Tommy. Escaping, the unlikely pair continue on their journey but before long the three villains ambush them and Avram is forced to kill one. The resulting anguish keeps Avram from presenting himself to the community leaders in San Francisco. He takes temporary refuge in a bar but runs into the last of the three villains, who challenges him to a gunfight. Avram is able to defeat the man without spilling blood, and takes his place in the community,

OPPOSITE: *As Mike Barnsby in* Force Ten from Navarone. BELOW: *As the outlaw, Tommy, who helps the rabbi Avram (Gene Wilder) journey across America in* The Frisco Kid *(1979).*

marrying Sarah Mindl's younger sister Rosalie (Penny Peyser) with Tommy as best man.

Ford worked hard to instil credibility as the bank robber with the heart of gold, but it was an uphill battle against Gene Wilder's histrionics in the title role. With so little to work with, Ford can only be congratulated for staying the distance.

What is so surprising is that a usually reliable director like Robert Aldrich could turn out such a turkey of a movie. Yet in the film business you're only as good as your last picture and the critics were unimpressed by such earlier Aldrich credits as *Whatever Happened to Baby Jane?* and *The Dirty Dozen*. Said one reviewer, 'Aldrich is stuck up the wrong turning he took with *The Choirboys*. Like that film, *The Frisco Kid* is based on the dangerous assumption that a number of comic episodes will add up to a comedy...one only hopes that his itch for comedy has been well and truly scratched.'

Ford's comments on the film have passed unrecorded, but *The Frisco Kid* will go down in the records as the last of the films that Ford should never have been involved in.

Over the next rise was Ford's return to the role that had made him a household name a few years earlier...Han Solo.

OPPOSITE: *Harrison Ford as Tommy, the well-groomed gunslinger in* The Frisco Kid *(1979)*.

CHAPTER 4

HARRISON FORD: RETURN OF THE HERO

. . . And Back Again

'I am very cautious of the word 'star'. I do my
job. I have been very lucky. Now I have to
figure out how to milk it without letting
it dry up.'
Harrison Ford

On March 7th, 1979, the Unit Publicist of *The Empire Strikes Back* released the following bulletin to the world's news agencies: 'American actor Harrison Ford has reached the snow stricken pass at Finse, Norway, to start work in *The Empire Strikes Back* in a manner to justify the claim that the show must go on.

'He arrived in the engine compartment of a snow-clearance vehicle, the only thing that could move along the Oslo-Bergen single track railroad which avalanches and collapsed snow tunnels have blocked.

'Ford had flown from London to Oslo to catch the train which travels a circuitous route across some of the most hostile winter terrain in Europe. At Geilo, a sizeable ski resort 30 miles east of his destination, the train was stopped in blizzard conditions.

'The railroad had decided to return its train to Oslo. But the film-makers needed Harrison Ford for scenes in the morning. So they radioed the train to unload the actor who then, by two improbable taxi rides, reached Ustaoset, just 23 miles from Finse. That was where the snowplough found him, to bring him along the track between 50 foot high snow drifts to Finse, which he reached at midnight.'

EMPIRE BUILDING

In retrospect, the makers of *The Empire Strikes Back* should have taken Harrison Ford's hectic arrival at the first location of the film as an omen of things to come. '*Empire* went about $6 million over budget,'

star Mark Hamill later said, 'and ten weeks over schedule, which drove George (Lucas) crazy because he doesn't like to see waste.' Lucas would have been particularly fearful of waste on *Empire*, as it was financed with his money, a fact he pointed out frequently to the cast and crew alike.

The script for *The Empire Strikes Back* was written by Lawrence Kasdan *after* he'd done the screenplay for *Raiders of the Lost Ark*. Kasdan explained the beginning of his involvement with the *Empire* project in the American magazine *Starlog*.

'I had absolutely no indication that my writing *Empire* was even being considered. Once I got the job I was excited because I liked *Star Wars* very much. I thought it was great art, in that *Star Wars* hooked into the archetypal images registered in our subconscious of how children perceive the world.'

Kasdan had been brought in after the death of respected science fiction and film writer Leigh Brackett. Before engaging Kasdan, George Lucas had completed a second draft, based on Brackett's first draft version. Kasdan had never seen the complete Brackett script. 'I only skimmed it. It was sort of old fashioned and didn't really relate to *Star Wars*. George had the story very well outlined, but there were sections in his script which, when I read them, made me say to myself, "I can't believe George wrote that scene. It's terrible." I later learned that George wrote stuff like that simply so that whoever wrote the next draft would know that a scene covering approximately the same kind of material that his

BELOW: *A rare moment of tenderness between Han Solo (Harrison Ford) and Princess Leia (Carrie Fisher) in* The Empire Strikes Back *(1980).*
OPPOSITE: *The principal players of* The Empire Strikes Back *(1980), Princess Leia (Carrie Fisher), Han Solo (Harrison Ford), Luke Skywalker (Mark Hamill) and Chewbacca (Peter Mayhew). (Lucasfilm Ltd).*

sequence dealt with belonged at that point in the script. My job was to take George's story and make it work through altering the dialogue and the structure. Naturally a movie is not a screenplay, but you can't make a good movie without a good script.'

HOW THE EMPIRE STRUCK BACK

As *Empire* opens we learn that the victory celebrations of the Rebel Alliance at the end of *Star Wars* had been a little premature. The Empire suffered only a temporary setback with the destruction of the Death Star. The rebels, presumably driven from their last outpost, have settled upon the ice planet of Hoth and are lying low, rebuilding their forces, for the all out conflict that surely lies ahead of them.

Darth Vader (David Prowse) and his forces are combing the Galaxy in a never-ending search for the rebels, launching robot probes towards any planets which look capable of supporting any kind of life at all. One of these probes lands on Hoth while Han Solo (Harrison Ford) and Luke Skywalker (Mark Hamill) are making separate patrols of the Rebel HQ's perimeter. Solo returns to the base, leaving Luke to make one more circuit. But Luke is attacked by a fierce native of Hoth, a Wampa, and hung up in the beast's lair as part of its provisions for the winter.

Meanwhile, back at the rebel base, a radio operator begins to pick up the probe droid's transmissions and Han and Chewbacca set off to investigate. The two successfully destroy the probe, but the abrupt halt in transmission makes the Imperial Forces monitoring the signals suspicious. Playing a hunch, Vader orders a full scale landing on Hoth.

By this time, Solo is concerned that Luke has not returned and, though darkness is falling outside, he sets off on a Tauntaun, a weird cross between a camel and a kangaroo, to search for his friend. Luke has managed to escape the clutches of the Wampa, but is finding it hard going on foot through the blinding snowstorms of Hoth. Luke collapses, overcome by the elements, but before he loses consciousness, he sees a vision of Obi-wan Kenobi (Sir Alec Guinness) urging him to seek out the Jedi master Yoda, who can be found on the swamp planet of Dagobah. And at that moment, Solo appears out of the swirling blizzard to rescue his friend.

Within hours, the Imperial Task Force is landing on Hoth, their huge armoured walking vehicles, AT-ATs (All Terrain Attack Transports), ambling relentlessly towards the Rebel Base. The Rebels initiate their well-rehearsed escape plan and begin to spacelift their soldiers and equipment off the ice-planet. As the Storm Troopers attack, Han and Princess Leia (Carrie Fisher), along with C-3PO (Anthony Daniels) are cut off from the main section of the base and are forced to make good their escape in the Millennium Falcon. Luke and R2-D2 (Kenny Baker) escape Hoth in a Rebel X-Wing Fighter, but rather than head for the Rebel rendezvous, they head for Dagobah, following the instructions of Obi-wan.

Han, Leia and Threepio discover that eluding the determined Darth Vader is not going to be as easy as they thought. The Millennium Falcon's hyper-space drive unit is acting up and Solo is forced to take refuge from his keen Imperial pursuers in a dense asteroid field. Solo hides the ship from Vader's forces by flying into a large cave in one of the larger asteroids. While Han and Leia attempt to repair the Falcon's damaged engines, the Imperial ships conduct bombing runs in an effort to flush out their quarry. Helping Leia with a particularly stubborn piece of equipment, Han takes advantage of their closeness to kiss her. But Threepio barges in and Leia, confused by her feelings, takes the opportunity to head for the Falcon's cockpit. Collecting her thoughts, Leia suddenly becomes aware that a horrifying creature has attached itself to the glass of the cockpit. Her scream alerts Solo to the fact that something is not quite right. He and Chewie venture out of the ship and discover that the walls of the 'cave' in which the Falcon is hidden have an organic look. Realising the danger at once, Solo orders Chewie back aboard the ship and immediately blasts the Falcon out. The 'cave' is actually the gullet of a huge space slug and though Solo escapes successfully, he still has to contend with the lurking Imperial Forces. Solo attaches the Falcon to one of the Imperial Star Destroyers, effectively vanishing the Darth Vader's radar screens. The Imperial fleet sweeps the area for a while, to no avail.

Meanwhile, aboard Vader's ship, the arch villain is addressing a group of bounty hunters, among them the notorious Boba Fett (Jeremy Bulloch). Vader offers a reward for the capture of Luke, Leia, Han and Chewie, but Fett is interested only in Solo. He means to deliver the space pirate to the criminal master-mind Jabba the Hutt to answer for an old debt.

Solo, still attached to the hull of the Star Destroyer, waits till the fleet is ready to blast into hyperspace. The Imperial ships release their refuse, then accelerate away. Solo detaches the Falcon at the correct moment and drifts, unnoticed by the Imperial Forces, with the garbage. Ingenious though Solo's ruse might be, Boba Fett knows that trick. As Solo plots a course for the nearest place he can think of with the necessary facilities to repair the ailing Falcon – the Cloud City of Bespin which is governed by his old friend, Lando Calrissian (Billy Dee Williams) – Boba Fett gives chase.

Luke, in the meantime, has found Yoda, an eighteen-inch tall alien with wizened features, and is working hard to improve his knowledge of the Force.

Back in Cloud City, which hovers at a dizzying height above the surface of the planet of Bespin, Calrissian's friendly appearance is finally belied when he leads Solo, Chewie and Leia into a room where Darth Vader and Boba Fett are waiting. The trio are taken prisoner and Vader orders that Solo is to be tortured, the idea being that if Han is caused enough pain, then Luke, with his knowledge of the Force, will be telepathically aware of his friend's plight and make a rash attempt at rescuing him. The torture proceeds apace until Vader, himself no slouch in the ways of the Force, is satisfied that young Skywalker is on his way. Then Vader turns Solo over to Boba Fett to be frozen in a block of carbonite for the return journey to Jabba's palace on Tatooine. If Solo's freezing is successful, Vader will similarly freeze Luke in order to deliver him to the Emperor himself. Solo is brought to the freezing chamber where Chewie and Leia wait, both bound. In the seconds before Solo is lowered into the freezing pit Leia blurts out, 'I love you!'

'I know!' replies Han laconically.

Luke arrives at Cloud City just as the frozen body of Solo is being loaded into Boba Fett's ship. He is unable to prevent the bounty hunter making off with his friend, and despite Leia's shouted warning about Vader's trap, engages his arch-enemy in hand-to-hand combat.

In truth, Luke is not properly prepared for the battle and is defeated by Vader in a dazzling light sabre duel, which ends with Luke losing his right hand, the weapon it holds and the battle. To cap his victory, Vader reveals that he is really Luke's father and entreats the young Rebel to join forces with him so that they may rule the Galaxy side by side. Despite what is a very attractive offer, Luke declines and leaps to what seems certain doom into a huge shaft which passes through the floating city and passes out into the rarified stratosphere of Bespin. Plummeting down the shaft for what seems like an eternity, Luke shoots through the end of the shaft and comes to rest, battered and bleeding, on an antenna on the underside of the city, several miles above the planet's surface.

In the meantime, Calrissian has convinced Leia and Chewie that he was forced to help Vader and the Empire under threat of the total destruction of Bespin and its inhabitants. The three agree to join forces and, after failing to stop the bounty hunter Boba Fett escaping with the frozen form of Han Solo, they make good their escape in the Millennium Falcon. But as they take off, Luke calls out to Leia telepathically and is rescued from his precarious perch.

Later, aboard the Rebel flagship, somewhere in deep space, Luke and Leia say goodbye to Lando and Chewbacca, who are setting off in the Falcon in search of Han Solo and the second chapter of the Star Wars trilogy closes leaving the audience with more questions than it had when the film began.

FILMING EMPIRE

After the nightmare George Lucas had gone through writing and directing *Star Wars* he decided that kind of involvement in so complicated a film project was simply more than he was willing to take on. His idea was to complete a rough draft of the script for *Empire* then turn it over to a professional writer for completion and polishing up. Then, with a professionally produced screenplay, he would turn his attentions to finding a director with the experience and the enthusiasm to helm the movie. He was looking for someone he knew and could trust to remain faithful to his original vision. He finally settled on Irvin Kershner, who had been one of his film teachers during his college days at USC in California. 'I knew George and (*Empire* producer Gary) Kurtz at the University of Southern California,' Kershner confirms, 'where I took courses and also taught. Through the years I occasionally saw them, but we weren't close friends.'

BELOW: *An unusual instance of tenderness between Han Solo (Harrison Ford) and C-3PO the talkative droid (played by Anthony Daniels). (Lucasfilm Ltd).*

Irvin Kershner, or 'Kersh' as he was called by the *Empire* crew, had originally started his working life as a professional musician. 'Before all this, I played violin and viola for chamber music and orchestras. I wanted to be a composer, originally, so I started with music. Then I went into art and photography. I travelled for the UN, UNESCO, for Syracuse University, for USC, for the State Department, and made hundreds of documentaries. I always did my own photography, until I began working in Hollywood.'

Kershner's film debut was with the 1958 film, *Stakeout of Dope Street*. From there he went on to direct such varied movies as *Loving* (1970), *Raid on Entebbe* (1977) and the John Carpenter scripted horror/thriller *Eyes of Laura Mars* (1978).

Kershner was brought in on the *Empire* project while Leigh Brackett was still working on her screenplay. 'She was about halfway through the script when I became involved,' said Kershner, 'and we decided to let her finish the thing before getting into meetings with her about the re-write – because I knew I'd want a re-write. So while I waited, I had discussions with George and some of the art people who were starting on the initial drawings, just sort of slowly getting started. And when she handed me the first draft, she said she was going into hospital that weekend for a check-up – and she never came out.

'So suddenly we had a first draft script on our hands and a definite start date for the picture on March 5th, 1979, which meant we'd have to get moving. So we took the script and started reading it and making a few changes – then George said, "You know, we've got to bring in a writer. Someone who is strong on dialogue and who can take on the burden of getting it whipped into shape." So we brought in

Larry Kasdan, and for months we would meet at my apartment in Los Angeles and go over it section by section. He would go off and re-write a section for a few days or a week, then he'd come back and we'd go over the pages he'd done, then he'd do another section. We did a very extensive re-write but it was still basically her script.

'When we'd polished it to the point that I thought it was now workable I came over to London and began pre-production, which for the first few months consisted of making drawings. I visualised and drew up the whole film to create the flow of it, to get the feel of the sets and the actual staging of scenes and even the cutting. It had to be very precise – so precise that drawings were made before the art director began to make the sets. Then we began to incorporate how the special effects would be done and I had to keep altering the drawings accordingly.

'It took about six months producing those drawings – we ended up with a book a foot thick. I sent copies to George and to all the technicians so everyone knew what they would be doing. With this book it was possible to get the flow of the picture established, which was the most important thing of all. Because as soon as you have a picture with a lot of gadgetry, blue screens, matte shots, super-impositions, etc. it tends to become very stiff if you're not careful. The actors become as stiff as the gadgets themselves.

'That was a major problem because the whole picture is special effects. People don't realise that almost every shot has something in it that's a special effect, and about half the effects were done completely on the set. Yoda, for instance was a total special effect and all done on the set. We added nothing to him later. Then there were the mechanical

OPPOSITE AND ABOVE: Dressed for the cold. Han Solo (Harrison Ford) saves the life of Luke Skywalker (Mark Hamill) yet again on the Ice Planet of Hoth. The Empire Strikes Back (1980). (Lucasfilm Ltd).

effects like the water effects and the fogs – there were so many things that we created right there...but, of course, there were many shots where I could shoot live action and then send the scene back to the studio in San Francisco for the opticals to be added. It was really a locked down situation on many of those shots. I mean, there were shots where we had to use the Vista-Vision camera (a special camera in which the film runs through the gate horizontally instead of vertically, giving a clearer image definition), it had to be exactly four-and-a-half feet off the ground, it had to be pointed no more than fifteen degrees up, the light had to come from the right, it had to be orange – all because of the special effects that would be added later – and then I could be free as I wanted within that frame.

'Then we reached the point where, in some shots, all I had was a completely black set and a few actors. It looked silly – nothing but a couple of lines drawn on the floor for the actors and that was it. I wouldn't see the finished scene for maybe six months after I shot it, then I get back a piece of film that's been married and the whole thing comes to life – it has a background and something flying around and other moving elements. It was a similar situation with some of the snow battle scenes – all I had were some men running towards me, smoke bombs, a few explosions and one man stumbling and falling in the foreground. And then the special effects team start working on it – they put in the three huge Walkers, which was a remarkable job, and then later they put in the laser blasts coming out of the Walkers, one of which hits the man I'd had fall over months before...so it was all working backwards.'

On the set, the director would find that scenes didn't work and would have to alter carefully storyboarded sequences at the last minute. And because of these alterations he was forced to give precious shooting days over to rehearsals of the new sequences and relighting of the sets.

The animatronic puppet that played the character of Yoda also proved to be one almighty headache. 'Actually there's very little of Yoda in the picture,' Kershner told Starburst's John Brosnan. 'and his scenes only took about ten days of filming, but they were very long days. He was monstrously difficult to work with and, on average, it took us three-and-a-half hours to shoot just two lines of his dialogue. The rehearsals took a lot of time too because we had a bank of TV monitors and three, sometimes four, technicians to manipulate Yoda. Frank Oz was coordinating it with me and we were both wearing earphones and mikes. The set was built four or five feet above the floor so we could have all kinds of mechanisms underneath Yoda...and it took endless rehearsals because you'd start and one of Yoda's eyes would go in the wrong direction or one ear would suddenly fall down, and I'd have to say, "Up with the left ear," or "Now take the left eye and move it around to the right...that's right, now focus it a little closer."

'Frank Oz would be watching the TV screens and I'd be watching the screens and the creature but we were the only ones who could hear what Yoda was saying. The crew and Mark Hamill heard nothing – they didn't know what was happening. Finally, we had to put a tiny earphone on Mark – a tiny miniature earphone with a very fine wire going back behind his ear so he could hear what Yoda was saying.'

Nevertheless the results were worth the bother. Yoda is a very convincing creation on the screen and the character won over the hordes of Star Wars fans instantly.

In the meantime, the problems that Kershner was experiencing were costing the production money. The 'Standing Still' budget (the money it cost to keep the production in business without shooting a single foot of film) was a staggering $100,000 a day. It was left to George Lucas to try to find the extra money from somewhere to ensure completion of the picture. Eventually he was forced to turn to 20th Century-Fox for help, something he wanted to avoid at all costs. And with the mounting financial pressures on The Empire Strikes Back, relationships between Irvin Kershner, George Lucas and Gary Kurtz became strained.

WORKING WELL

Yet through all this, Harrison Ford had only good things to say about Irvin Kershner. 'He was wonderful,' Ford enthused. 'He's a different kind of director. But we also had a very close relationship on the level of freedom to contribute.'

Kershner, a director sensitive to the needs and talents of his actors, encouraged every contribution Ford was willing to make.

'Occasionally, I feel very sure about the changes,' says Ford, 'like the "I love you,""I know" scene. I knew that my last speech had to be a strong character line. I convinced Kersh to give me the "I know" decision and I'm grateful he did. When George finally saw the sequence cut together, he said, "It's a laugh line. I'm not sure it belongs there. This is a serious, dramatic moment."

'I said, "I think it really works." and Kershner agreed with me. So George said, "Okay, go with it."

'From what I've seen and heard, the "I know" line really does work. It relieves a grim situation without generating laughs or diverting the drama. It also serves to make Solo's plight more poignant and memorable.'

Harrison Ford has no qualms about altering a line of dialogue that a writer might have spent months on if he feels it will improve the end result.

'Writers sometimes have to live with a script so long,' he says firmly, 'that it begins to suit them too well – they can't see the validity of changes.'

Lawrence Kasdan wasn't too happy with some of the changes that had been made to his script – sometimes on the very day of shooting. 'Han and Leia's relationship is not at all what I had envisaged,' Kasdan told the American magazine Starlog. 'I could be the only person who feels this way, but I thought their romance had a touch of falseness about it. Han and Leia's scenes were among what I was proudest of in my script, but they hardly remained. Their being changed had a lot to do with the circumstances of filming, Kershner and the actors' feelings about doing their roles again. I was one of the people who wasn't crazy about Harrison Ford in Empire.'

When Empire Strikes Back opened in America on May 21st, 1980, Star Wars fans across the country had been queuing for three days. The film recovered its cost three months after that and eventually went on to pull in nearly as much in ticket sales as the original Star Wars movie. Not bad for a film that caused just about everybody connected with it too many sleepless nights.

GOOD PRESS, BUT...

The critics' reception of *Empire Strikes Back* was only a little short of a standing ovation. Yet many did point out that the ending of the film was no ending at all and smacked of the same kind of thinking behind the cliff-hanging endings of the old Saturday morning serials – a cheap shot to get the audiences back for the third part of the trilogy. Harrison Ford took a defensive stand over such comments and answered them smoothly.

'I have no real defence for that argument,' he admitted, 'but what obligation is there to tie up every question with an equal answer? The cliff-hanger is because the trilogy was really constructed in the classic form of a three act play. Naturally, there are going to be questions in the second act which have to be resolved in the third. I guess it really depends on what you go to a movie for. I figure there was at least eleven dollars worth of entertainment in *Empire*. So if you paid four bucks and didn't get an ending, you're still seven dollars ahead of the game.'

There's no denying Ford has a point.

The accusations that *Empire* was too serial-like could have been an omen of Ford's next project. Though he didn't know it at the time, Harrison Ford would go on to star in George Lucas's homage to those same Saturday morning serials in the brilliant thirties adventure movie, *Raiders of the Lost Ark*.

CHAPTER 5

HARRISON FORD: MATINEE IDOL

From the Stars to Star

'Harrison Ford is more than just an actor playing a role in *Raiders of the Lost Ark*. He was involved in a lot of decision-making about the movie as we went along. And this wasn't by contract, it was because I sensed an exceptional story mind and a very smart person and called on him time and again.'
Steven Spielberg, director of
Raiders of the Lost Ark

'The little film that George Lucas and Steven Spielberg decided to make together is growing by the minute. Shooting begins of *Raiders of the Lost Ark* on May 15th, 1980 at George's happy hunting ground of Elstree Studios – and already, before a single shot is completed, they have four sequels in the planning stages.' was how British fantasy film magazine *Starburst* announced the start of work Lucas's follow-up to the *Star Wars* saga in February, 1980. The report gave Lawrence Kasdan as the script writer, Frank Marshall as producer, but no hint as to the cast.

Before long, rumours were circulating that *Raiders of the Lost Ark* was not a new project at all, but the third part of the *Star Wars* saga. Said *Empire Strikes Back* producer Gary Kurtz of that idea, 'I can categorically deny that. It's not science fiction at all. It's a Thirties action adventure type story about a search for a lost treasure. A typical Clark Gable, soldier-of-fortune kind of movie.'

No more news issued from the Elstree set of *Raiders* until the movie opened in America on May 25th and at London's Empire (where else?) cinema on July 30th, 1981.

WHO ARE THE RAIDERS OF THE LOST ARK?

It is 1936. Though the Second World War has not yet begun, the Nazi military machine is readying itself. Hitler, fascinated by the occult, has agents scouring the globe for all manner of magical artifacts.

Indiana Jones, professor of archaeology and 'procurer' of rare treasures, is on an expedition to Peru, in an effort to obtain a solid gold idol hidden in the bowels of the Temple, crossing bottomless pits, avoiding a hail of poisonous arrows and outrunning a huge rolling boulder before emerging into the daylight again with his prize. Unfortunately for him, a rival archaeologist, Belloq (Paul Freeman) is waiting at the entrance of the Temple with a horde of kill-hungry Hovitos warriors in tow. And it's the idol that Belloq and his primitive pals are after. Jones hands over the idol but makes good his escape. Chased by the Hovitos, Jones heads for the river and the seaplane that's waiting for him. Jock (Fred Sorensen) the pilot manages to get the plane into the air in time. But Jones is not out of trouble yet. Slithering around his feet in the cockpit he finds 'Reggie', Jock's pet snake. And Jones hates snakes.

Back in the United States, Indiana Jones – now looking decidedly different from his leather clad, unshaven adventurer persona in a sober tweed suit and spectacles – is visited by his old friend, Marcus Brody (Denholm Elliot), who is also the curator of the National Museum in Washington. Brody had brought along a couple of government agents, Col Musgrove (Don Fellows) and Major Eaton (William Hootkins), who need some help. The government men have intercepted a Top Secret communication from Berlin to the German Embassy in Washington. It seems that the Germans are excavating the ruins of Tannis but still need an ancient relic, the headpiece of the Staff of Ra to complete their work. And the last man who was known to possess the piece is another

BELOW: *Indiana Jones, the scholar, peruses ancient markings on the headpiece to the Staff of Ra with an elderly Jewish scholar in Cairo.* OPPOSITE: *Indiana Jones the hero captured in the closing scenes of* Raiders of the Lost Ark *(1981). (Lucasfilm Ltd).*

old friend of Jones's: Abner Ravenwood. Jones explains that Tannis is the legendary resting place of the lost Ark of the Covenant, the chest in which the children of Israel kept the pieces of the tablets Moses brought down from Mount Sinai. The Nazis are apparently after the Ark, believing that an Army that carries the Ark before it would be invincible. Whether that's true or not, the American authorities can't afford to take any chances and Jones is engaged to retrieve the Ark before the Nazis.

No sooner has Jones accepted the assignment than the Nazis are on his trail. Jones first must head for Nepal, in search of Ravenwood and the vital headpiece. Arriving at 'The Raven', a sleazy bar on the foothills of the Himalayas, Jones finds Marion Ravenwood (Karen Allen) beating a huge Australian climber in a drinking match. Marion is less than thrilled to see Jones and tells him that her father, Abner, died a few years earlier leaving her stranded in this terrible place. Jones offers her money in return for the headpiece, but is asked to return the next day. After Jones leaves, another interested party, the Nazis, arrives to talk business for the headpiece. They are led by a thoroughly unpleasant Gestapo man called Toht (Ronald Lacey). When Marion proves uncooperative, Toht brings some of his persuasive powers to play. He is going to burn the headpiece out of Marion with a red-hot poker.

But in the nick of time, Indiana Jones comes through the door, whip flying, guns blazing to rescue Marion from the bad guys. And in the ensuing battle, 'The Raven' is burnt to the ground, and everything Marion owns with it. From now on, she and Jones are partners in the quest for the lost Ark.

Arriving in Cairo, Jones and Marion team up with an Egyptian digger, Sallah (John Rhys-Davies), to get to the Ark before the Germans. But the Nazi spies are hot on the trail, and in a rousing battle, in which Jones defeats hordes of unsavoury Arabs, finally shooting the largest, Marion is kidnapped and apparently killed when Jones causes the truck carrying her off to crash and explode. But the mission must go on. Soon, Jones has located the Ark and, as he and Sallah lift it from its centuries old hiding place, the infernal Belloq arrives on the scene to snatch Jones's treasure from under his nose again. But fair exchange is no robbery, and the Nazi gives Jones something in return for the Ark: Marion.

Jones and Marion are to become eternal prisoners in the Snake-infested pit called the Well of Souls, while the Ark is spirited away by Belloq for extensive tests before being turned over to the Fuehrer in Berlin.

Jones escapes his prison by crashing a huge statue through one of the walls. When he learns that the Ark is being placed on a plane, Jones manages to sabotage the aircraft, forcing the Nazis to return to Cairo by road. Jones gives chase and in a spectacular, stunt-laden sequence once again takes possession of the Ark.

Jones and Marion load the Ark onto the America-bound ship, the Bantu Wind, and say goodbye to their friend Sallah. But a few hours out of port their ship is intercepted by a German submarine. Belloq

OPPOSITE: *Indiana Jones (Harrison Ford) sweeps Marion Ravenwood (Karen Allen) off her feet in the Well of the Souls.*
ABOVE: *Marion tells Indy that they're partners as her bar burns around them. (Lucasfilm Ltd).*

once again has the Ark, and this time, Marion too. Jones escapes detection and hitches a ride on the back of the submarine. The sub arrives at a small island, where Belloq plans to carry out his tests, and the Ark is unloaded. Jones is always nearby.

The Ark is carried into the interior of the island by the Nazis, who are still holding Marion prisoner. Jones is captured and forced to watch while the triumphant Belloq opens the Ark. But Belloq's triumph turns to terror as he, and Jones, come to realise the true extent of the power of the Ark as the hand of God wipes the slate clean.

FROM THE SANDS OF HAWAII TO THE SANDS OF THE SAHARA

The apocryphal tale of *Raiders'* genesis was reported both in Dale Pollock's *Skywalking* (the George Lucas biography) and in Tony Crawley's *The Steven Spielberg Story*. Both books told of Lucas's retreat to the Hawaian beaches to forget the horrors of making *Star Wars*, and of Spielberg's joining him there with the news that *Star Wars* had been a monumental hit. Over a sandcastle, the world's two most successful film-makers hatched a plot to make a movie that would mix the mythic qualities of the Occult and the derring-do of the Saturday matinee serials and out-Bond Bond in the process. The co-author of the original story of *Raiders*, Philip Kaufman, was

originally slated to direct, but when he dropped out of the project, Spielberg stepped in.

At this stage, the project still had no writer. Until Spielberg introduced a young Chicago advertising copywriter, Lawrence Kasdan to Lucas. Spielberg had read a screenplay by Kasdan called *Continental Divide* and was trying to acquire it to produce for himself.

'When Spielberg first read it,' said Kasdan, 'he told my agent', "I'm doing a movie with George Lucas and I think this guy would be great to write it. Would it be all right if I showed George *Continental Divide*?" And we, of course, agreed. Then I came in and met George – he had read the script and liked it – and at that first meeting, George hired me to write *Raiders*.'

Lucas, Spielberg and Kasdan spent a week thrashing out the basic plot of *Raiders*. These sessions were preserved for posterity on tape and at the end of the week Kasdan went off to write the first draft script.

'I left those meetings feeling I was in pretty good shape and then sat down and realised, Uh-oh, this is going to be hard!' said Kasdan. And hard it was, at least hard enough to keep the young writer occupied for a full six months.

Finally, Kasdan took the finished script in to show Lucas. What happened next came as something of a shock. The scriptwriter working on *Empire*, Leigh Brackett, had died suddenly. Lucas desperately needed a writer to take over. Could Kasdan handle it? 'But you haven't even read *Raiders*, yet,' protested

BELOW: *Indiana Jones at the home of Salla (John Rhys Davies) 'The Best Digger in Egypt.'*
OPPOSITE: *A portrait of Harrison Ford as Indiana Jones. (Lucasfilm Ltd).*

Kasdan. Lucas only smiled. He was following his instincts – which were rarely wrong.

Meanwhile Spielberg had read Kasdan's *Raiders* script and was delighted. 'Larry didn't stick with our story outline one hundred percent,' commented Spielberg, 'A lot of the movie is Larry's own original ideas, his characters. George provided the initial vision, the story and the structure of the movie. Then George and I together provided key scenes throughout the film. And Larry essentially did all the characters and tied the story together, made the story work from just a bare outline, and gave it colour and some direction.'

With the script in the safe hands of Lawrence Kasdan, Lucas and Spielberg could turn their attention to who was to play the key role of Indiana Jones.

The auditions for the movie were to be held at Lucasfilm's West Coast offices. 'We wanted an unknown, originally – a total unknown. Conceitedly, George and I wanted to make a star out of Johnny the Construction Worker from Malibu. We couldn't find a construction worker in Malibu, so we began looking at more substantial people in the film industry.'

Both Lucas and Spielberg had a picture in their mind's eye as to the kind of hero they were looking for. Lucas saw Jones as a scruffy playboy. The kind of adventurer who, on duty, dressed like Humphrey Bogart in *Treasure of the Sierra Madre*, complete with leather jacket, brown fedora and a bullwhip.

Spielberg's Jones was more of a grizzled alcoholic, gruffly romantic and ruggedly handsome.

Their first choice for the role was TV actor Tom Selleck. Selleck was enthusiastic but aware that the new pilot he was working on might turn into a full series for American television. The pilot was *Magnum P.I.* It did turn into a full series and Selleck was out of the running.

'We were stuck,' said Spielberg. 'We had three weeks left to cast the part of Indiana Jones, and there was nobody close. Then I saw *The Empire Strikes Back* and I realised Harrison Ford *is* Indiana Jones. I called George Lucas and said, "He's right under our noses!" George said, "I know who you're going to say!" I said, "Who?" and he said, "Harrison Ford! Let's get him." And we did!'

According to *Skywalking*, Harrison Ford had read the script for *Raiders* shortly after Kasdan had finished it but had remained cool towards the project. 'They could find me if they wanted to,' Ford is quoted as saying. Nevertheless Ford must have known that the part was perfect for him. 'It was clearly the most dominant single character in any of George's films,' said Ford, 'quite in variance with his theories about movie stars and what they mean.'

Despite his enthusiasm for the project, one aspect of *Raiders* bothered Ford. 'My only immediate reservation about playing Indiana Jones,' said Ford, 'was that in the script the character was a little bit like Han Solo. Steven Spielberg and I wanted to make

BELOW: *Fightin' mad. The baddies carry Marion away and Jones gives chase.* OPPOSITE: *When he catches up with the kidnappers, Jones blasts away with his trusty revolver, only to cause the truck to overturn and explode. (Lucasfilm Ltd).*

sure that the characters were spread apart. We did that by making use of the opportunities that existed in Lawrence Kasdan's screenplay.'

Time was too short for a re-write of the script. Yet Spielberg recognised in Ford a native ability with dialogue and wanted to implement some of Ford's suggestions. What happened was like a scene out of *Let's-make-a-movie* movie. 'The production was based in London,' said Ford, 'and Steve and I sat on the plane from Los Angeles and went through the script, line by line, for ten hours. By the time we got to Heathrow, we'd worked out the entire film.'

It's just as well that they had, for no sooner had Spielberg and Ford arrived in Britain than the entire cast and crew were whisked off to La Rochelle in France to spend the first five days of the movie's shooting schedule filming the submarine hijack of the Bantu Wind. It was during these five days that Ford was to get his first taste of the stunts he would be required to perform in the course of portraying Indiana Jones. 'Swimming to the submarine didn't involve danger,' said Ford 'it only involved discomfort.' The worst was yet to come.

Star Wars had put the phrase 'special effects' into everyone's mouth. Suddenly, after *Star Wars* opened, reviews were peppered with the words. It was as though George Lucas had invented the concept all by himself. With *Raiders*, Lucas was to elevate another previously ignored movie art to star status. Stunts.

Much was made, at the time, of the fact that Harrison Ford did many of his own stunts for the film. 'Hell,' he quipped, 'if I hadn't done some of the stunts in *Raiders*, I wouldn't have been seen in the movie at all.' Yet strangely Ford is no kind of keep fit freak. 'People always ask me how I keep in shape. Every time the question comes up, I can manage to sneer. It's a common enough question, considering *Raiders*. And I say, being in movies is enough exercise for me.'

In reality, Ford was lucky enough to have some of the best stuntmen and stunt directors in the business working with him. Stuntmen are always used for the most dangerous 'gags' for the simple reason that if the star of the film were to hurt himself and hold up shooting, hundreds of thousands of dollars would be wasted.

'There were some very capable stuntmen doing some of the action bits, but I probably did a good deal more action stunts than an actor normally would do. That was important because we wanted to have our fights always be character fights, instead of just having whatever spectacular event a stuntman could come up with. Indiana Jones fights in a certain way, which Steven (Spielberg) let the stuntmen and me choreograph. Some of Indy's battles are incredible. "How can Indy possibly do all this?" We had to take the edge off that with a bit of humour and at the same time not make fun of the material. So Indiana Jones had to be a character with a sense of humour. It's Indy's way of looking at life that makes our fights unique!'

Glen Randall was the stunt co-ordinator on *Raiders*. Says Randall, 'They talk about the dangers

ABOVE: *Indiana Jones translates the Egyptian hieroglyphs he finds in the map-room of the City of Tannis.*
OPPOSITE: *When in doubt, shoot it out. Harrison Ford wields a mean handgun in* Raiders. *(Lucasfilm Ltd).*

stuntmen go through, wrecking cars and airplanes, but I think the stunt that gets the most people hurt in this industry is the simple fight routine. When you throw a punch, you're throwing it with all the force you'd normally use to hit someone, but you're missing them by inches. There are a lot of stuntmen who just cringe when they find out they've got to do a fight with an actor who's not had a lot of experience doing them – 'cos nine times out of ten, they're going to get hit!'

One of the most spectacular thrills in *Raiders* is in the opening sequence when Indy races the giant rolling boulder for the exit in the Temple. It was Ford himself outracing the rock. 'Looked a little scared that scene, didn't I? I'd have to have been crazy not to be. It wasn't a *real* boulder, but it wasn't cardboard, either. It took 800 pounds of plaster to make it roll right. And if I had tripped, I could have been in big trouble. The director thought at first we ought to use a stuntman – but I thought I could do it and Glen Randall, our stunt coordinator, agreed. We all felt the more action scenes I could personally do, the easier it would be for the audience to identify with and believe in the character. But if I didn't trust the stunt guys who were manning the safety devices and looking out for me, I never would have done it. No way!' The scene was shot from five different angles, twice from each angle. 'So Harrison had to race the rock ten times,' said Spielberg. 'He won ten times and beat the odds. He was lucky. And I was an idiot for letting him try!'

Indy's escape from the Well of Souls provided an opportunity for the film makers for a really spectacular stunt. In an effort to break a hole through the wall of his prison, Indy topples a huge statue of a jackal god and rides it as it falls, a tip of the hat, perhaps, to Slim Pickens' riding the Atom Bomb to his last round-up in *Dr Strangelove*. Harrison Ford, intrepid but not stupid, knew the time to step aside for professional stunt double Martin Grace.

As Glen Randall explained, 'The Jackal was 28, maybe 29, feet high. Plaster of Paris but still incredibly heavy. And we put big hydraulic rams on one leg and hinged it at the bottom so we knew exactly the plane it was going to fall in. It could only fall one way, if everything went right. We had a huge breakaway wall for it to fall through.'

But for all the planning, something went wrong as the stunt was filmed. If you watch closely during this scene in the movie, you'll see Indy lose his footing for an instant as the statue begins to topple. 'Yes, it went too soon,' agreed Martin Grace. 'And that's when you have to think very fast. I was actually still hanging down when it started going. I should have been actually on my position. . . Stunt people are usually very fast thinking people. In situations like that you have to think very fast and get it together. We've got sort of lightning reflexes, very sharp minds and that's a great combination to come up with the goods.' Grace emerged unscathed.

But with Ford doing so many of his own gags, it's no surprise that he had a couple of near misses himself.

'There's a scene where I run through the jungle,'

Ford told an American magazine, 'swing on a vine, let go the vine, fall into the river, grab onto the pontoon of a seaplane that's taxi-ing, get onto the wing and climb into the cockpit as it was taking off – and the plane crashed on take-off.'

Of course Ford wasn't hurt. But it does show that no matter how careful you are, accidents will happen.

Harrison Ford must have been on a lucky streak during the filming of *Raiders*. He had had another near miss on location in Tunisia during the shooting of the Tannis Dig sequence. Ford told the story to the American fan magazine, *Prevue*. 'Indy has a fight which takes place in and around the propellors of a Flying Wing airplane. The engines are running full tilt and one set of wheels is chocked, so the plane's going round in circles. The bad guy is supposed to throw me down in front of the wheels and I was supposed to roll over backwards to get away from the wheels.

'All day long the technical crew was having trouble with the plane. It weighed a couple of tons, so they were powering it with low-gear, high-torque electric motors – the kind that can push through a brick wall without slowing down. They had to stay out of camera range, at the end of a cable 50 yards away.

'I still wanted to do the fight myself. I'm able to add bits of character touches to moments like these, and when the audience recognises the actor, it adds credibility to what is normally straight action stuff. We rehearsed the scene several times, then decided to shoot it.

'Everybody's ready and the take begins. I go down and start to roll away – and my foot slips, right under the rolling plane's tyre.

'Everybody was yelling, "Stop! STOP!" while the tyre crawled up my leg. Luckily the brakes worked – inches before my knee was crushed – but I was pinned to the sand.

'I'm not normally a worrier, I know they're not going to kill the main character in a twenty million dollar film. I also know Indy wouldn't look good with a peg-leg. I was a lot more careful about stunt work after that!'

And he'd have to be. Still to come was the hazardous chase in which Indy starts by leaping from a horse onto a speeding German truck, which is coincidentally carrying the Ark, and ends with our hero falling from the front of the truck, crawling hand over hand beneath the vehicle, then being dragged for a couple of miles down the road in the dirt before climbing up the tail board. You'd think for that Ford would insist on a stuntman. He did, and he got one. . .for the long-shots. In the close-ups, there was Ford, hanging onto the rear of the truck, scraping up the gravel road on his belly. As usual, Ford was dismissive. 'It couldn't possibly be dangerous,' he said at the time, 'because I have a few more weeks shooting the picture.'

Being so closely involved in so many of the gags on *Raiders* has given Harrison Ford a stuntman's outlook as far as 'falls' are concerned. 'The stuff that always turns out to be dangerous is the stuff nobody thinks about. It's not the dangerous stunts – which you think about, protect yourself, calculate and worry about, so that you take the danger out of it – it's the stuff you *didn't* think was dangerous that sneaks up on you.'

'SNAKES. WHY DID IT HAVE TO BE SNAKES?'

Most people would think that an actor who also did so many of his own stunts, like Harrison Ford, would have enough on his plate in a film like *Raiders of the Lost Ark*. Not so. The folk who made *Raiders* knew that the more severe the trials suffered by the hero, the more the audience would be rooting for him. Also, a hero with a failing seems more vulnerable and more easy to identify with for an audience. So the film makers gave Indiana Jones a fear of snakes and needless to say, Indy met more than just a few snakes during his adventures in *Raiders*. The Well of Souls was filled with them.

'Steven Spielberg kept wanting more and more snakes,' said Ford, 'but he had to make do with six thousand garden and grass snakes flown in from Holland, and used bits of garden hose to fill the spaces the boas and pythons couldn't.'

Fords's co-star, Karen Allen, wasn't mad about doing the scene in the Well of Souls at first. 'Harrison has on his boots and gloves, and leather clothes, and I have naked arms and nothing on my legs or feet. In the beginning it was tough, because I just couldn't stand the snakes on my feet. But I got used to them.'

Producer Frank Marshall, who shot some of the snake footage, wasn't wild about reptiles, either. 'I had to cure myself of a common phobia of snakes. But once you see other people, like a snake handler, not worry about it, then you touch one. Then I got to be real comfortable with them. Some of the shots I did were a real challenge. Snakes aren't afraid of anything, they'd even go right into the fire. So we had to invent a way to get them to stay away from the fire.'

Though most of the snakes used in the scene were harmless, the crew did use a couple of cobras, whose bite can kill, to add a little real danger for Indy.

'When we used the cobras,' recalled Howard Kazanjian, the film's co-executive producer, 'we had a hospital gurney on the set, and outside the stage we had ambulances with open doors. On the end of the gurney was an open medical kit with a hypodermic needle placed into the phial of serum from India.' Ford was in good hands.

Harrison Ford dismisses Indy's fear of snakes with his characteristic easy smile. 'They don't bother me at all. When I was a kid, I worked in a boy scout camp as a nature councillor, I used to collect them. Used to run and catch every snake we could. And I'm amazed that that's the most frightening scene for most people.'

But, as I said, all heroes must have a failing. There *is* something the intrepid Ford doesn't like. 'Spiders!' he told *Movie Star* magazine. 'Not because they're creepy, but inside my house they multiply, and then their kids have kids. Ugh. All those spiders all over the place.'

One particularly gruesome scene in *Raiders* does just happen to have a few spiders in it. The scene in the Temple in Peru. But unlike the scene with the snakes, it was the spiders that had to be watched out for rather than their human co-stars. 'It's funny how people think tarantulas are so dangerous,' said producer Frank Marshall, 'when in fact they're very fragile creatures. If they fall or you drop them, they die. You have to be very careful with them. We did lose one of them one day when two got in a fight – a battle to the death.'

But for Ford, it was the snakes that had the last laugh: shortly after the opening of *Raiders*, Ford told author Tony Crawley of a strange incident. 'Back home,' said Ford, 'just the other week – you're not going to believe this – I got bitten by a damn snake in my garden!'

'I PUT AS MUCH OF MYSELF INTO THE CHARACTERS AS POSSIBLE.'

The only other thing Harrison Ford had to do in *Raiders of the Lost Ark* was portray the character of Indiana Jones. Director Steven Spielberg had nothing but praise for Ford's abilities as an actor. 'Harrison is a very original leading man,' said Spielberg. 'There's not been anybody like him for 30 or 40 years. In this film he is a remarkable combination of Errol Flynn in *The Adventures of Don Juan* and Humphrey Bogart as Fred C. Dobbs in *Treasure of the Sierra Madre*. He carries this picture wonderfully.'

Ford was well aware of what was expected of him. 'It's a question of responsibility to define the character for the audience, to make the film as good as you can.'

But he had a good ally in Steven Spielberg. 'Steve allowed a kind of collaboration that was really a lot of fun for me. I like to become really involved as much, and as long, as possible. If I had a little bit of an idea, Steve added to it, and then I added to it, and then he added to it, and it built into something we both thought was better than before . . or so stupid we

BELOW: *Harrison Ford as Indiana Jones.* OPPOSITE: *Jones and Marion take their leave of their friend Salla and are passed into the tender care of Ktanga, a kind of latter-day pirate.* (Lucasfilm Ltd).

both ended up rolling about on the floor with laughter.'

And, in the spirit of Indy's line in the movie, 'I'm making this up as I go,' Ford and Spielberg were making changes to the script even during actual shooting.

'My only impulse to change lines comes when the words are impossible to get out of my mouth,' said Ford. 'The process of film making involves so many situations and personalities that it becomes a very liquid medium. The physical presence of actors and crew are concrete factors, but the script should relate to them more like a road map of probabilities than a rigid blueprint.'

The biggest change Spielberg and Ford made to the script was to delete the 'Sword vs the Whip' duel that was written as a climax to the battle in the marketplace in Cairo. In the film, Indy comes face to face with a giant of a swordsman. The swordsman performs an intricate routine with a huge scimitar. Indy, unimpressed, pulls out his revolver and shoots him. Not sporting, but efficient.

'I was in my fifth week of dysentery at the time,' recalled Ford later. 'The location was an hour and a half drive from where we stayed. I'm riding to the set at 5.30am, and I can't wait to storm up to Steven with this idea. I'd worked out we could save four whole days on this lousy location this way. Besides which, I think it was right and important, because what's more vital in the character's mind is finding Marion. He doesn't have *time* for another fight. But as is very often the case, when I suggested it to Steven – "Let's just shoot the sucker" – he said, "I just thought the same thing this morning." Sure, the idea was nothing. Putting it on film, that's the most difficult part.'

That scene also told the audience much about Indiana Jones. The world weary expression on Indy's face as he draws his gun, sums up the character's directness. As Ford explains, 'Indy is a kind of swashbuckling hero type, but he has human frailties. He does brave things, but I wouldn't describe him as a hero. He teaches, but I wouldn't describe him as an intellectual. I wanted to avoid any elements in the role that might be too similar to Han Solo. But Indy doesn't have any fancy gadgetry keeping him at a distance from enemies and trouble. The story is set in 1936, after all, and he's right in there with just his battered trilby and a bull-whip to keep the world at bay.'

STAR!

'All I care about is good acting,' George Lucas was once quoted as saying. 'Star value is only an insurance policy for those who don't trust themselves making films.' But when *Raiders of the Lost Ark* opened in America on July 12th, 1981, that's exactly what Harrison Ford had plenty of.

'There's more excitement in the first ten minutes of *Raiders*,' said *Playboy's* Bruce Williamson, 'than any movie I have seen all year. By the time the explosive misadventures end, any moviegoer worth his salt ought to be exhausted.'

Just about all the reviews were of the same opinion. *Raiders* was a masterpiece of popular cinema. 'Surely destined to go down in history as one of the great, fun movies,' said Britain's trade journal, *Screen International*.

'*Raiders* represents Spielberg's best work in years, a return to the briskness and coherence that have been missing since *Jaws*,' said *Time* magazine.

Ford himself was happy about his involvement in the film and the end result.

'*Raiders* is really about movies,' he explained. 'It is intricately desgined as a tribute to the craft. I'm quite in awe of the film, and the way it was accomplished. Steven set out to make an epic film, technically complex, on a short schedule. He finished twelve days early and under budget. He didn't waste any time in retakes. Steve was very fast and efficient, and that's the way I like to work.'

Yet his experience on *Raiders* did leave Ford with one cautionary thought 'I occasionally wonder how much longer I can perform in heavy action roles,' he told an interviewer. 'Working in sub-zero blizzards and 130 degree deserts is incredibly demanding, physically. Sometimes I think the most difficult part of being in films is being cool as an airplane rolls over your leg – and acting like it doesn't hurt at all.'

As Harrison Ford's next film project drew closer, his attitude had mellowed a little 'With me,' he said, 'the last film is always the toughest. I'll soon be down on record as saying *Blade Runner* was the toughest.'

OPPOSITE: *A portrait of Harrison Ford as Indiana Jones. (Lucasfilm Ltd).*

CHAPTER 6

HARRISON FORD: ACTOR

From Artisan to Artist

'Harrison has an immense understanding of the entire movie making process. You can't fool him at all. He always knows exactly what is happening. His contributions were tremendous, on a story level as well as to his own character. He brought many ideas to me. In fact, it got bloody embarrassing. They were so good, there was no way I could wriggle out of using them.'
Ridley Scott, director of *Blade Runner*

The release of *Blade Runner* in May, 1982 (September, 1982 in Britain) marked a definite attempt by Harrison Ford to change his image. The fan following built up by such lightweight vehicles as the *Star Wars* pictures and *Raiders of the Lost Ark* were puzzled by the singular lack of humour in Ford's performance. So much so that they stayed away in droves. *Blade Runner* was not a commercial success.

But *Blade Runner* was perhaps Ford's most important film. Certainly, it was his first opportunity to sustain an *acting* performance in a starring role. The insight and depth he brought to the character of Rick Deckard showed that Ford was capable of far more than the wisecracking characterisations of Han Solo and Indiana Jones would lead one to suspect.

More than that, the backdrop against which the drama of *Blade Runner* was played out, although futuristic, was grittier and more realistic than the fantastic environments of Indy and Solo.

THE FANTASTIC WORLD OF BLADE RUNNER

Earth, Winter 2019. It is the twilight of Human Civilisation. Those who have sufficient health and wealth have long since departed the planet for the off-world colonies. Those who remain, the poor, the sick, live in huge mega-cities, amidst the towering, monolithic skyscrapers. Demolition is uneconomic. New structures are simply erected over the existing buildings. The streets, with their flashing neon signs, bizarre traffic jams and seething inhabitants are like an urban planner's nightmare.

Spinners, flying police cars, whir through the air. There is as much life above the streets as in them.

Genetic engineering has become a boom industry. After most of Earth's animals became extinct, the genetic engineers scored big by creating artificial animals for a pet-hungry populace. Soon, the science had reached a level of sophistication where artificial humans were just as easy to produce as the animals. These creatures were supplied to the off-world colonies as slave labour and to the military for combat duties in deep space.

The Tyrell Corporation, a sort of brand leader of the replicant business, introduced the Nexus 6 model, several years before the story takes place. These top-of-the-line models have several times the strength and intelligence of their creators, but are almost indistinguishable from them. For this reason replicants are outlawed on Earth. And it is the task of paid bounty hunters, the blade runners, to exterminate any replicants discovered on the home planet. The business of telling a replicant from a human is a tricky one, undertaken with the help of a kind of sophisticated lie-detector, a Voight-Kampff machine.

The story of *Blade Runner* begins when Los Angeles police receive reports that a group of Nexus 6 replicants have seized control of a space shuttle, killed the crew and are headed for Earth. The officer in charge of the investigation, Captain Bryant

ABOVE: *Rick Deckard on the mean streets of Los Angeles, 2019AD.* OPPOSITE: *Man versus replicant in a world gone mad. (Ladd Co).*

(M.Emmet Walsh), sends for the only man who has the remotest chance of tracking down the creatures – Rick Deckard.

Deckard is arrested at a noodle bar on one of the bustling streets of the metropolis by Gaff (Edwards James Olmos), a cop with aspirations to better things, and is flown directly to Bryant's office in a police spinner. Bryant blackmails Deckard into tracking down the four replicants, and sends him to the headquarters of the Tyrell Corporation to question the legendary Tyrell (Joe Turkel) himself. Arriving in Tyrell's huge office, Deckard is greeted by the beautiful Rachael, Tyrell's executive assistant. Tyrell suggests that Deckard try his fancy machine on Rachael before he will agree to help. At first, Deckard can't understand the results he's getting with his Voight-Kampff test. But after close questioning he's sure. Rachael is a replicant.

Elsewhere, Roy Batty (Rutger Hauer) and his three replicant companions, Leon (Brion James), Zhora (Joanna Cassidy) and Pris (Darryl Hannah), are hatching a plan to prolong their short lifespans – a failsafe device built into all replicants so that if they do get out of control, they only have a limited time to do whatever damage they can.

Deckard trails the replicants to a seedy, downtown hotel. Though his prey has fled, Deckard finds some kind of animal scale in the hotel room's bath. The scale is identified by a street vendor as coming from an artificial snake, manufactured locally. Deckard then questions the man who made the snake and discovers that the replicant animal was sold to an exotic dancer who works in an up-market strip joint. Investigating this lead, Deckard recognises the dancer as Zhora, but when he confronts her, she fells him with a devastating blow. Zhora attempts to strangle Deckard, but is interrupted. The girl flees and Deckard, shakily, gives chase. He pursues her into the teeming streets of the metropolis and eventually gets a clear shot at the fleeing replicant, blasting her flailing body through several plate glass windows before she finally falls.

But the 'termination' is witnessed by another replicant, Leon, who traps Deckard in an alleyway and proceeds to beat him savagely. Just as Leon is about to gouge out Deckard's eyes, a gunshot rings out. Rachael has trailed Deckard out into the streets and saved his life by mere seconds. The body of Leon crashes to the ground, lifeless.

Deckard and Rachael return to his apartment.

After spending a few hours together, Deckard and Rachael are irresistably drawn to each other and they make love.

Meanwhile, unknown to Deckard, Batty has gained entrance to the Tyrell Corporation's headquarters and is confronting Tyrell with his demands for a prolonged life. When Tyrell is unable, or unwilling, to help, Batty murders his 'creator' and flees the scene. But Deckard is soon back on his trail and the chase leads to a final confrontation in a derelict building which towers above the Los Angeles skyline. Deckard barely survives the encounter, and it seems that Batty, at the last minute, sacrificed his life to allow Deckard to live. Deckard has no idea why Batty allowed him to live and will probably never find out. But he must now contend with the fact that Rachael is considered an illegal replicant and decide whether he should disobey his orders to retire her.

Deckard returns to his apartment and the sleeping Rachael. The two then flee the building and the city and set off for a new life in the unspoiled countryside that lies beyond the Metropolis.

DO ANDROIDS DREAM OF ELECTRIC SHEEP?

No matter how skilled a film's performers and technicians are, unless the blueprint from which they work, the script, is tightly crafted, the final movie will suffer as a result. In the beginning was the word. Most movie people agree that just about all the problems encountered during the shooting of a film can be traced back to difficulties left unresolved by the scriptwriter.

The script of *Blade Runner* was based, loosely, on the novel *Do Androids Dream of Electric Sheep* by respected science fiction author, the late Philip K.Dick, who died tragically on March 2nd, 1982, shortly before the completed film of *Blade Runner* was released.

The need for the script to be 'right' is so universally recognised by film makers that it often takes longer to produce a screenplay that everyone is satisfied with than it does to shoot the actual film. *Blade Runner* is no exception. Work began on the transfer of Dick's story to the screen almost ten years before the film was released.

'It all began years ago,' Dick told *Starlog*. 'Martin Scorcese and Jay Cocks were both interested in *Androids*, but they didn't option (purchase the film rights to) it. That was the first movie interest in any property (story) of mine. Then later, Herb Jaffe optioned it and Robert Jaffe did a screenplay back about 1973. The screenplay was sent to me and it was so crude that I didn't understand that it was actually the shooting script. I thought it was a rough. I wrote to them and asked if they would like me to do the shooting script, at which point, Robert Jaffe flew down here to Orange County. I said to him then that it was so bad that I wanted to know if he wanted me to beat him up there at the airport or wait until we got to my apartment.'

The Jaffes made little progress with their attempts to put *Do Androids Dream of Electric Sheep* on the big screen. But the Jaffes weren't the only film folk interested in the project. Some time in 1974, Hampton Fancher approached Dick with a view to obtaining the film rights to the novel, but as the rights still rested with the Jaffes, Dick was unenthusiastic. Then, in 1977, the Jaffes let their option on the film rights lapse and within a year, Fancher and his partner Brian Kelly found themselves in possession of the film rights for Dick's novel.

Kelly approached Michael Deeley, Oscar winning producer of *The Deer Hunter* with a view to raising finance for further development, but the reception was cool. Deeley felt that there would be too many problems involved in translating Dick's complicated story to the big screen. Nevertheless, Kelly and Fancher persevered. Fancher produced an eight page outline for the film which so impressed Deeley that he encouraged the partners to come up with a full script. 'I hadn't ever intended to write the screenplay myself,' Fancher recalled, 'but I was convinced that this was the only way to get the project off the ground.'

'Lord knows,' commented Dick, perhaps uncharitably, 'I didn't think much of his screenplay.' But despite Dick's reservations, Kelly and Fancher took their script to Deeley once again. 'He loved it,' said Fancher.

Deeley began to hawk the script around the production companies in Film City. 'People were interested,' said Fancher, 'but they wanted changes. They'd want a happy ending or they'd want something else changed. It was pretty precarious there for a while. I think there were about four or five drafts written before Ridley Scott came into it. When Ridley came in that sort of wrapped it up because of the *Alien* reputation. That's what it needed for the studio to get down to business with it.'

On the strength of Ridley Scott's participation, Michael Deeley had put together a deal with Filmways. At this point the title of the project had changed from *Do Androids Dream of Electric Sheep* to *The Android*.

At the time Scott was approached to direct *Blade Runner*, he was scheduled to helm Dino De Laurentis' multi-million dollar adaptation of the best-selling series of *Dune* novels by Frank Herbert. But delays in the production made it possible for Scott to squeeze *Blade Runner* in before beginning work on *Dune*. (For the record, *Dune* has since been filmed under the guiding hands of the team director David Lynch and cinematographer Freddie Francis).

What was it about the script that convinced Ridley Scott to take on the project? 'What appealed to me, having just done *Alien* which was very interesting, was the involvement in just developing that future environment further. I love that whole process, almost as much as any other part of movie making. I just didn't want to step off onto ordinary ground again. What I felt was great about the script was that it was dealing with the near future. It had to be a familiar city, which it is. A lot of aspects of that city are familiar right now. In fact, a lot of people who will see the film, will experience that kind of future themselves. I also liked the aspect that there was a real character in there, rather than a two-dimensional cardboard character, which happens too often with science fiction films. Because the film is usually dominated by a monster or event the characters do, essentially, take second place.'

After Ridley Scott was signed to direct, a major revision of the script, by now called *Dangerous Days*, began. Initially, Fancher was resistant to some of the changes proposed. And as a co-owner of the project,

Fancher was in a position to dig his heels in. But pressure to alter portions of the script became so great that Fancher realised the only way out of the situation was to bring in another writer.

Enter: David Peoples.

As Fancher remarked later, 'I was surprised when I got Peoples' script. Those things that Ridley had wanted that I thought couldn't be integrated into the script had been rendered by Peoples in ways that were original, tight and admirable. I really liked it. But we never actually collaborated. He came in on very short notice and he had a lot of work to do, but he did it very fast and very well.'

Peoples had been brought into the project during November 1980. Shooting was still several months away. 'I read the script,' said Peoples, 'and immediately felt that it was so good that I was disappointed, because when they came to have a meeting I told them I couldn't make it any better. It was a terrific script. I don't know which ones Phil Dick read that he didn't like, but certainly the one I read was absolutely brilliant. And that was the one I worked from to make the changes Ridley wanted, to make it more his vision.'

Throughout this process of re-writing, Ridley Scott kept a watchful eye on the developing script. Another title change was instigated.

'The final title actually came from an obscure science fiction paperback (by Alan Nourse),' Ivor Powell, the associate producer told me. 'This paperback had something to do with doctors in the future, when doctors and medicines are banned. There are all these illegal doctors who go out to administer medical help to the sick, and the people who supply them with instruments when they run out are called blade runners. Hampton Fancher gave that name to Deckard in his script as a code-name. I'm not sure whether it was Hampton or Ridley who came up with the idea of calling the film *Blade Runner*.'

Dutifully, the film makers bought the rights to Alan Nourse's *Blade Runner* novel, only to discover that there was another book of that name by William Burroughs. Originally Nourse's novel was to be filmed and Burroughs had been hired to adapt the script. But when the movie fell through, Burroughs had his version of the story novelised and published in book form. *Blade Runner's* producers were forced to purchase the rights to that version of the story, too.

In the meantime, David Peoples was running into problems. During his revision of the script many of the sets and vehicles were either under construction or already built.

'One time I changed a scene,' said Peoples, 'and

BELOW: *Deckard interviews one of the replicant suspects, Zhora, who has been working as an 'exotic dancer' in a sleazy downtown bar. (Ladd Co).*

somebody said, "Jesus, you wrote the ambulance out!" I said, "So what?" and they said, "Well, it's already built."'

Peoples gives full credit to Ridley Scott as the true architect of *Blade Runner*. 'If anybody was authoring it at this stage it was Ridley. He was dominating, supervising and caring about what went on here. Then, down the line, Harrison Ford and Rutger Hauer made some really nice contributions in the way of dialogue. I would sometimes be writing a scene that Ridley would be shooting the following week, and twice I guess, I was writing stuff that was going to be shot that day.'

Harrison Ford's involvement in *Blade Runner* goes back further than that of David Peoples. 'They first asked me about *Blade Runner*,' said Harrison Ford, 'when I was doing. . . hmm, *Empire*, I guess (I have such a bad memory). They were going to make it in London at that point in their plans and I said, "Well, thank you very much, gentlemen, but I don't want to work in London any more. I want to go home." Five of my last eight films have been made in London. When they came back to me, it turned out that they couldn't put it together in London for some reason.'

That reason was intertwined with the collapse of Filmways and the involvement of Tandem Productions and The Ladd Company.

I asked Ivor Powell to explain the ins and outs of the move. 'After getting Filmways in as the major and the distributor, the next problem was how to shoot the film. Despite all the location scouting we did, there was no one place that had the concentration of architecture that was right. As always, with a film like *Blade Runner*, it comes down to how you are going to crack the script, how you're actually going to make it work, how the logistics are going to work and how they are going to work within a price. The budget was gradually being pushed up and Filmways, I guess, were being carried screamingly along with it, and though we were unaware of it at the time, they were having tremendous cash-flow problems. They believed in the project, but I don't think they had the money for a twenty million dollar movie. The budget had gone from about twelve or thirteen million dollars, which was totally impractical, right up to twenty million plus. Finally, Filmways collapsed and Michael Deeley, very cleverly I think, turned the film around to Tandem Productions (the company of Jerry Perenchio and Bud Yorkin) and The Ladd Company in a very short space of time, though we went through a terrible hiatus where we were trying to hold the crew together. The directors' strike was looming for later that year. We knew if we didn't start the movie by a certain date, we would never start at

BELOW: *Deckard stalks around the darkened innards of the Bradbury Building in search of the last two replicants, Pris and Roy Batty. (Ladd Co).*

all. It was one of those pictures that you *knew* that if it didn't get made then, it would never get made at all. It wasn't every director's cup of tea. Finally, the cash-flow started and we got off. We had, at that time, attempted to do a budget. I'd done a quick budget, which had come in at seventeen or eighteen million dollars, if we were making the picture in England. But if we'd made the move to England, it would have been too late to beat the director's strike, which ironically never happened anyway. So for that, and some other reaons, we made the movie there, at the Burbank Studios.'

With the production base re-located to Hollywood, Harrison Ford once more became available for the leading role as Rick Deckard, blade runner. But for many of Ford's fans, *Blade Runner* was a radical departure from the kind of film that had endeared their hero to them. Ford was following his oft-stated intention to avoid type-casting and ensure that each of his roles was sufficiently different from the last.

Ford was finally signed for *Blade Runner* while the finishing touches were being put on *Raiders of the Lost Ark*. And, as with *Raiders*, Ford was not the film-makers first choice for Deckard. I asked Ivor Powell why Harrison Ford had been picked for the role. 'By popular demand, really,' said Powell. *Raiders of the Lost Ark* hadn't come out then, so we didn't know if it was going to do well. At one time, we were even talking to Dustin Hoffman, and that would have been a totally different picture. Dustin is not a macho character and he asked Ridley, "Why the hell do you want me to play this macho character?"

'Ridley was searching for more than just a superficial, macho film,' continued Powell. 'He wanted a real character in there, and Dustin, as I understand it, put forward some wonderful ideas. But it wasn't the film we were talking about making. Finally, I think it just came down to the fact that Harrison fitted the bill.'

Ridley Scott also told me that, as far as he was concerned, Harrison Ford was the man for the job. 'He has a very unusual quality that shines through in two pictures, *The Conversation* and *Apocalypse Now*. It's a strange, slightly sinister, side. Very low-key and sombre. Almost a different Harrison Ford. Very dangerous. It fitted the nature of both Deckard and the film very well. The only other actor we saw for the part was Dustin Hoffman. He was looking for a different kind of movie. But, god knows, I'd like to work with Hoffman some day. After things fell through there, we went straight to Harrison. He'd been under consideration from the beginning.'

And at the beginning, Ford seemed pleased to be

BELOW: Deckard tentatively explores Sebastian's apartment looking for the last two replicants on his hit list. (Ladd Co).

involved in the project 'I'm preparing to start work on *Blade Runner*,' he told an American fan magazine, shortly before *Raiders* opened. 'I'm sure I was considered for the film as a result of *Star Wars*, just as Ridley (Scott) proved his capabilities in this genre with *Alien*.

'I can't complain so far. *Star Wars*, *Empire*, *Raiders* and *Blade Runner* are classy, high-quality melodramas, not pot-boilers. They all contain currents of intelligence and morality, and are handled with taste. I'm looking forward to *Blade Runner*. I think I can give it an aspect that will set it apart from *Raiders* or *Star Wars* or anything else I've done.'

And while on a trip to Britain to promote *Raiders of the Lost Ark*, Ford had apparently brought his enthusiasm for *Blade Runner* with him. As he told the British magazine, *Films*, '*Blade Runner* is an important step towards more serious roles. And I think it will be a very commercial film because of its unique vision. But I was serious about it because of the people involved and was happy to find out that Ridley was interested in developing the density of the characters as well. I felt that we could work together to present a character who was interesting and very different to anything else I've done until now.'

Ford and Scott laboured long and hard to achieve something they could be proud of. 'We have a lot of discussions about scenes,' said Ford during filming, 'but not about motivation. I don't ask him what my motivations are and he doesn't ask me what they are. The discussions are usually about practical matters – what we're trying to get out of a scene, what the obligations are on him as master of the story and me as the character. Then we look for common ground to accomplish the story points and the character points at the same time. And sometimes that's done without any discussion at all, and sometimes we discuss all hell out of it!'

This process was underlined by Ridley Scott. 'There is always a period of rehearsals before the film, and I at least try to get a couple of weeks for casting and reading through the script. I usually take a certain amount of time and tell the actors about the overall film, not just about their particular parts. It's usually a lengthy process, but then it is worth it because they know how they sit, how they figure within the overall piece. It is very important that they understand the entire thing.'

Ford was also aware that the characters must be clearly defined before the first shoot of film ran through the camera. 'Ultimately it is the actor who

OPPOSITE: *Harrison Ford, out of character.* BELOW: *With Sean Young in the touching love scene in* Blade Runner. *(Ladd Co).*

has to perform the act and commit it to film. So, while a director's job is incredibly complicated and difficult, there are elements that are never resolved – how a prop should work, whether the character carries his gun here or carries it there. These may be simple little details, but they are only decided when somebody gets a strong attitude about things and begins to form a point of view. The character Deckard does finally. He begins to develop a point of view about the circumstances around him.'

Yet for all this there seemed to be a fundamental difference between Deckard as Ridley Scott saw him and the character as envisaged by Ford. Scott's Deckard was apparent to the director as far back as the Hampton Fancher versions of the script. 'It started to emerge for me,' said Scott, 'that Deckard was a kind of Philip Marlowe character, which is an obvious comparison. Harrison figured he should go for utter reality, almost like de Niro's Travis Bickle in Taxi Driver.' Ford himself saw Deckard as, '. . .a reluctant detective who dresses like a middle-aged Elvis Costello. He's a skilled investigator, an expert in his field, but he's a little out of practice when the movie opens. He's lost his motor drive. Exterminating people, even non-human ones, is not something he likes to do, and he's not comfortable with authority. He's very tough, but he's no match for a top-of-the-line replicant.'

Tough though Deckard may have been, he didn't seem to be quite tough enough to resist the aspect of Chandler-esque pastiche that was creeping into the movie. Under Scott's direction, *Blade Runner*

seemed to be taking shape as a kind of homage to the great black-and-white noir movies of the Forties. As the film's director of photography, Jordan Cronenweath, told *American Cinematographer*, 'Ridley felt the style of photography in *Citizen Kane* (1940) most closely approached the look he wanted for *Blade Runner*. This included, among other things, high contrast, unusual camera angles and the use of shafts of light.' All the film lacked at this stage was a punchy voice-over narration delivered in the kind of lazy drawl made famous by Humphrey Bogart. 'The generation of the idea of a voice-over came very quickly,' said Scott. 'Eventually a screenplay was written with a voice-over very much in mind.' Ford wasn't happy at the prospect of a voice-over narration, but for the time being kept his counsel. There was still the problem of being able to satisfy the requirements of the script without compromising his own goals and principles.

'My object,' Ford told an American fan magazine, 'every time out of the gate is to contrast the public's last known impression of me. So, with *Blade Runner*, I'm working against *Raiders of the Lost Ark*. They originally wanted Deckard to wear a big felt hat. I told them I had just finished wearing one in *Raiders*, so we changed that.'

Despite evidence to the contrary, Ford felt that the science fiction content of *Blade Runner* was minimal. 'I wouldn't call *Blade Runner* science fiction,' he said, 'because it's much different from the public's conception of sf, based on movies they've seen in the past.' Granted, but *Star Wars* was actually less

OPPOSITE: *Battered and bleeding, Deckard doggedly refuses to give up his search for the illegal replicants.*
ABOVE: *Ford is directed by Ridley Scott in the Bradbury Building battle scene. (Ladd Co).*

worthy of the tag Science Fiction than *Blade Runner*. 'There are special effects in it,' he continued, 'but they're kind of throwaways. From a technical point of view, *Blade Runner* is not an effects film, but I'm sure Doug (Trumbull)'s work will add a great deal to the story.'

And even at this early stage, Ford was aware of the film's noir potential. As he told the reporter of *Movie Guide*, '*Blade Runner* is a big city detective story, the kind Raymond Chandler might have written, but it takes place in the future. It's realistic and gritty and takes place entirely on Earth.'

Still, for all the confusion over what *Blade Runner* and Deckard were all about, Ford was enjoying working with Scott. At least for the time being. 'Ridley's very particular and demanding in all elements of the production. I knew he was a great visual stylist, but I was glad to find depth and subtlety of character.'

THE FILMING

The filming of *Blade Runner* finally got under way on March 9th, 1981, after a year of preproduction planning and an additional fourteen weeks of constructing and dressing sets. The project was already running three months behind schedule.

Actual locations, both in the United States and in Europe, had been considered by the film's producer, Michael Deeley. But finally, the idea of location filming had proved both impractible and undesirable. The production team were happy to settle for shooting the exteriors on the Warner Brothers New York street set, which had been used for such earlier detective yarns as *The Maltese Falcon* (1941) and *The Big Sleep* (1946) as well as more recent fare like 1982's *Annie*.

Industrial designer Syd Mead and *Blade Runner*'s production designer Lawrence Paull had been hard at work for twelve months creating the backdrop against which the drama would be played. The cast had been assembled and carefully coached in the lore of *Blade Runner*. The on-set smoke machine was switched on. The real work could begin.

Most of the action in the movie takes place at night. This meant the cast and crew knuckling down to a gruelling, hours-of-darkness shooting schedule. Lunch was called at midnight and the 'day's' work ended at four or five in the morning. Scott and his key cast and crew members had to survive on an average of four hours of sleep a night, which prevented the kind of family atmosphere Ford had been used to on the Lucas films.

Unlike Lucas, who delegated many of his responsibilities as a film-maker, Scott preferred to be personally involved in every aspect of the process. Reports filtered through to the trade publications that Ford and Scott weren't getting along. These reports hinted that Ford was unhappy with Scott's attention to the mechanics of film-making, a fascination that ran to the extent of Scott operating his own camera during key scenes, a charge Ford denied. 'It was no big bone of contention between us,' said Ford. 'I don't think he ever got around that problem. He just learned to accommodate the reality. Ridley was able to shoot a few things he really wanted to. And he's very good. Especially with the hand-held camera. I think there's quite a few shots in the film with Scott operating his hand-held camera. He likes to watch the performance through the lens. As an actor, I'm glad he wasn't able to do that all the time. I think it's better to have his attention on other things. He knows that's the way I feel. I think that when a director is looking through the camera, he's watching the edges to be sure where everything is. I want a director to be helping me with a whole scene, the performance. It's not that this isn't possible, or that Ridley hasn't done it before. . . and very well.'

Ford kept himself pretty much to himself during the seventeen weeks of shooting. His co-star Sean Young would have welcomed more collaboration between them. 'I think Harrison is probably an all-or-nothing type of person and he can't really relate to other cast members full out, because he feels he might become too wrapped up, and by being friendlier with the crew, he can avoid that whole mess.'

Rutger Hauer was less open in his views on working with Ford. 'I only had two moments in the film with Ford,' he said. 'I didn't work that long with him, but he was fine. Our scenes were very clearly written in the script. I didn't feel there was a problem of communication because we didn't have to talk about it. It was just a matter of doing it without getting hurt.'

As was his custom on his other films, Ford did most of his own stunts for *Blade Runner*. One memorable scene had him clinging precariously to a ledge, hundreds of storeys above the teeming streets. 'We were using a 65mm Mitchell camera,' explained effects man David Dryer, 'which weighed about 75 pounds. With that kind of weight cantilevered out over Ford there was always the chance that the camera would break a casting and come right down on him. So we rigged a special plate and support to get the camera actually looking back down on itself.'

It was Rutger Hauer's job to haul Ford up onto the roof. 'Harrison didn't want to fall down that twenty foot drop, or whatever it was. So he was hanging there, with a wire for support, but it was still kind of tough to get him up.'

But Ford was dismissive of the danger involved. 'That shot where I'm hanging from the girder. . . well, God knows, I'm not hanging 30 storeys above the ground there. Not only am I not hanging from the girder, I've got a safety belt on and a wire that's got me clipped to the bottom of the girder. . . and I'm *acting* like I'm hanging from a girder, from the contortion of my face, the sweat of my brow. That's all acting. . . *wonderful* acting!' But on a more serious note Ford is careful to draw a clear distinction between what he does and 'real' stunts. 'What I've done in *Raiders of the Lost Ark* and *Blade Runner* is 'physical acting'. Stunts are falling off a tall building or crashing a car. Something you're silly enough to think isn't going to hurt the next day.'

Meanwhile, rumours abounded that Ford had drastically altered his appearance for the movie, one American Newspaper even claiming Ford played Deckard with a shaved head. 'The crewcut was my idea,' said Ford. 'And I had to talk Ridley into it, because he was afraid that it might make me less gorgeous. The haircut couldn't be done unless Ridley was there. It took about four hours to get it. With long pauses for consideration by Ridley. My ambition was always to get it right down. Real short. I wanted to give the impression of a character who has given up on himself, was unconscious of his appearance and had lost, to a large degree, that ego that keeps us all doing things like combing our hair, brushing our teeth and all of that. I thought it was important to suggest that and change my appearance in some way. I think it's more interesting for an audience, even if they know right away who it is. They don't have the same expectation of you if you don't look the same. It gives you a foot forward.

'And one of the other things that drives me nuts when doing a four month shooting schedule is when someone is fiddling with your hair between every shot. I just can't stand that. It just drives me nuts. If I could have short hair on every film. . . I mean, some of my best friends are hairdressers, but it does drive me nuts. The first thing I do after a film where I have long hair is cut it all off.'

The beard was also Ford's idea. 'The first day of *Blade Runner*, I'm shaved. When the events begin to take over my life, it hardly seems a proper time to shave. . . when things are going the way they are in *Blade Runner*, there doesn't seem time for a bath and a shave. I think that kind of detail goes to make up the character. I try not to lose sight of those little things.'

By this time, Ford had had a chance to think through Deckard's relationship with Rachael. 'It's clear that Deckard doesn't think very much about women at all,' he told the author of *Blade Runner* souvenir magazine. 'He's the type of guy that would see them occasionally but not have any use for them around the house. He has a wife and child but they seem to have gone in search of a better life. Deckard

acknowledges on Rachael's first appearance that she is attractive. But then she becomes a puzzle and, when he figures out she is a replicant, he seems to have no further use for her. He sees Rachael as a zero. But her display of emotion, even though he knows it's false, implanted, pulls him out of his despair. As he begins to become involved with her, he is forced to confront what is really going on around him.'

THE RELEASE

Director Ridley Scott called 'cut!' for the last time on *Blade Runner* during the second week of July, 1981. The production was already over-schedule and over-budget. The film makers busied themselves with such vital post-production activities as editing, dubbing and adding the excellent Vangelis music. The following January, the first of the *Blade Runner* trailers was released in America. It featured scenes from the movie under the music of the Inskpots, enhancing the idea of *Blade Runner* as a 1940s pastiche.

A rough cut of the film previewed in Denver Colorado. Fans seemed unhappy with the abrupt ending of Deckard and Rachael stepping into the lift and the doors slamming shut behind them.

'It was fairly apparent that the crowds didn't care for this,' observed Scott. 'Fortunately, we had also shot an alternative ending, with Deckard and

BELOW: *'One side, folks, I'm a cop!' Deckard moves in to examine his own handiwork after the killing of Zhora, first of Deckard's replicant victims. (Ladd Co).*

ABOVE: *Harrison Ford as Rick Deckard stalks the Bradbury Building (Ladd Co).*
OPPOSITE: *Ford, in his street clothes.*

Rachael leaving the city together in a Spinner, heading towards the unpolluted Northwest.' Also at this stage, there was no Harrison Ford voice-over to explain the more ambiguous scenes in the film. I was lucky enough to see this version at an early preview in London around March, 1982, and feel this 'first draft' to be far superior to the final release cut.

When the film was released on June 25th, 1982 in America, the 1940s look and the laconic (some would say, 'bored') narration was singled out by the critics as the chief target for attack. Ford was a little defensive about such comments. 'I thought it had the makings of a very original film,' he said. 'It was no ambition of mine to play the character like a Forties Bogart figure, but it was always on Ridley's mind. It was always my hope that there wouldn't be a voice-over, that we wouldn't need one. I thought the character needed to be a representation of a certain type of physical environment, the result of that kind of life. The voice-over was always Ridley's idea, from the beginning.'

Scott was a little more philosophical. 'We never addressed the problem of the voice-over early enough,' he told me. 'I wanted the voice-over from the beginning. The screenplay was written with a voice-over.' But that wasn't the voice-over that appeared in the finished film. And Scott was far from happy with the end result. 'The voice-over is an essential part of the Marlowe-type character of Deckard and also to a degree helps clarification. One of the most interesting aspects of *Apocalypse Now* was the voice-over. It was incredible. I think Coppola went on for nearly six months trying to get that right. I think, with hindsight, I would have re-done the voice-over in *Blade Runner*, and I think Harrison would as well.'

As it turned out, the final narration was no masterpiece and it jars against the other aspects of the production. Of particular note was the corny speech over the scene in which replicant Roy Batty dies. Ford's tired voice proclaims. 'I don't know why he saved my life. Maybe in those last moments he loved life more than he ever had before. Not just his life. Anybody's life. My life. All he'd wanted were the same answers the rest of us want. Where do I come from? Where am I going? How long have it got? All I could do was sit there and watch him die.' Raymond Chandler it *isn't!*

Almost predictably, the reviews weren't good. *Playboy's* Bruce Williamson thought *Blade Runner* was a 'major disappointment' despite 'smashing production values and fine actors' and summed up

the movie saying, 'by the time Ford and Hauer face off for their climactic showdown, *Blade Runner* had grown dull – a simple case of Philip Marlowe meets Frankenstein.' The British trade publication *Screen International* felt 'the special effects dominate the film while the plot and characters fade into the background,' and pointed out that 'in spite of his voice-over ironies, Rick Deckard is no Philip Marlowe.' The American trade bible *Variety* said that 'Ford's frequent inertia mutes the detective angle of the story which is couched in some hard-boiled Chandleresque narration and in the long run proves to be the weakest aspect of the pic.'

Some critics believed that the level of violence in *Blade Runner* was more explicit than was necessary. Ford countered this in his usual eloquent style. 'There's a really unfortunate and ill-advised attitude to the violence in the film. I am conscious of violence in a film. I abhor it when it is used for the sake of itself. I was anxious to make sure this character represented the abhorrence of violence. And he does. He wanted to get out of the police force because he couldn't stand the killing. After every incident of having to kill someone, the character's revulsion is clear. And, ironically, he is not killing human beings. That's what the thematic backbone of the film is. They're not really human beings. And yet, his empathy with something that looks like a human being – which is later to lead him into a romance with a machine – affects him.'

In spite of the negative criticism of the film, Ford's performance was praised. Script-writer David Peoples was enthusiastic about Ford's portrayal of Rick Deckard. 'Harrison is an absolutely magnificent actor,' he commented. 'He's amazing. He's like the great old guys. He becomes Deckard. I mean, you don't see him act like Deckard, he *is* Deckard and Deckard is different from Han Solo and entirely different from Indiana Jones. In *Blade Runner* he's a seething guy with a lot inside him. He's a guy who's got a lot of problems, who's holding a lot in, and Harrison does it brilliantly.'

Science fiction author and friend of Philip K.Dick's, Norman Spinrad was more restrained about Ford's performance. 'Harrison Ford is fine in the rather undemanding role of Deckard.' Yet for all this, *Blade Runner* was an extremely important step in Ford's career. It was his first opportunity to show what he could do as a serious actor. It was beginning to become obvious that Ford was a far better actor than his *Star Wars* and *Raiders* vehicles allowed one to see. But further expeditions into the area of serious acting would have to wait. Already the date for the beginning of principal photography of the third part of the *Star Wars* saga was approaching. It was almost time for Ford to return to the worlds of robots and rayguns as Han Solo in *Return of the Jedi*. But not before he'd rested up a while. 'It would take an Act of Congress to get me to work before *Jedi*,' he said, 'I haven't had six months with the kids for a long time.'

CHAPTER 7

HARRISON FORD: CONTRACT PLAYER NO MORE

From 'Get me Harrison Ford' to 'Get me a Harrison Ford type!'

'Harrison Ford is a pure cinema actor, there is nothing theatrical about him – it's just him. He doesn't mind if his shirt's out or his hair's ruffled or his profile isn't beautifully lit. What matters is what he's doing, what he's expressing, what the camera is covering. He works beautifully with the camera.'
Richard Marquand, director of
Return of the Jedi

The close of *The Empire Strikes Back* left Han Solo (Harrison Ford) sleeping the sleep of the living dead, frozen in a block of carbonite and on his way to the palace of Jabba the Hutt, an alien criminal mastermind, to suffer the penalty for dumping a cargo of illegal spices belonging to Jabba. Some of the more imaginative *Star Wars* fans put this fact together with the knowledge that Harrison Ford had only signed for one *Star Wars* picture at a time and began to circulate rumours that neither Ford nor Solo would be appearing in the third *Star Wars* film, *Return of the Jedi*.

But shortly after the release of *Raiders of the Lost Ark*, Harrison Ford went on record in the American magazine *Starlog* to put paid to such wild speculation. 'If I hadn't been able to do some of my other movies I might have felt differently about doing *Return of the Jedi*. As it stands, I'm delighted to be coming back. Han, Luke and Princess Leia were created to tell this story, so I'm glad to be in on the third act.'

Yet, just *how* Han Solo would return was a closely guarded secret. Nobody involved with the production would talk without the express permission of *Star Wars* creator George Lucas. Then Lucas himself broke the silence in a pre-*Return* interview – though he was giving nothing away. 'The original (*Star Wars*) idea kind of got segmented, and the fact that the story is a fairy tale got lost, especially in the beginning, because the science fiction took over. I think that *Return* for better or worse, is going to put the whole thing in perspective.'

RETURN OF THE SOLO

The planet Tatooine, where the *Star Wars* saga began. Across the desolate landscape trudge the two robots, R2–D2 and C–3PO, on their way to the palace of Jabba the Hutt with a message from Luke Skywalker. The two are admitted to the palace by Jabba's sinister henchman, Bib Fortuna, and are brought before a slavering slimey slug-like creature – the Alien Crimelord, Jabba the Hutt. A hologram image of Luke shimmers into existence and the message begins. Jabba is asked to return the carbon-frozen body of Han Solo to his friends. Young Skywalker feels that he and Jabba can reach an agreement which will be mutually beneficial and as a token of his good will he makes a present of the two droids to Jabba.

The Alien Crimelord reacts with disdain. There will be no bargain. R2–D2 is put to work on Jabba's sailbarge, while C–3PO is to become his interpreter.

Later, a party in the Palace throne room is

BELOW: *Han Solo (Harrison Ford) and Princess Leia (Carrie Fisher) defend themselves from Imperial attack at the very portal of the second Death Star's defence shield power plant in* Return of the Jedi *(1983).* OPPOSITE: *Han Solo, Princess Leia and Luke Skywalker (Mark Hamill) on the Ewok planet of Endor. (Lucasfilm Ltd).*

ABOVE: *Han Solo (Harrison Ford), Luke Skywalker (Mark Hamill) and Chewbacca (Peter Mayhew) are dragged before Jabba the Hutt's throne. (Lucasfilm Ltd).*

interrupted when the bound figure of Chewbacca the Wookie is hauled before Jabba by a diminutive bounty hunter. The bounty hunter demands a reward for the capture of Solo's co-pilot and to add force to his argument, threatens to detonate a bomb unless his demands are met. Jabba is amused by this rogue and strikes a bargain. Chewie is led away to Jabba's dungeons. Finally, the party winds down and through the silent, darkened Palace, the bounty hunter moves towards the frozen body of Han Solo. Releasing Solo, the bounty hunter reveals 'his' identity. . . Princess Leia Organa. But Jabba has been expecting just such a trick and armed guards escort Solo to join his Wookie friend, while Leia becomes the favoured slave of Jabba.

Before long, Luke Skywalker arrives at the Palace and appears before the criminal emperor. He demands the release of his friends or Jabba must face the consequences. Supremely confident, Jabba packs Luke off to dinner with his pet Rancor beast. Except that Luke is the dinner. Using only his natural agility, Luke defeats the monster, upsetting Jabba, who decides that the only fitting fate for Luke and his friends is to be thrown into the Pit of Sarlacc, a giant sandworm which digests its prey alive.

Arriving at the Pit aboard Jabba's sand barge, Luke gives the criminal one more chance to bargain. Jabba, not in a conference mood, gives the order to hurl Luke into the pit. Then all pandemonium breaks loose. R2–D2 hurls Luke's light sabre high into the air, the young Jedi knight catches it and the fight is on. In a dazzling battle, Luke and his team

defeat Jabba and his followers, including the bounty hunter Boba Fett, and head into space.

Han, Leia, Lando and C–3PO set off to meet up with the remains of the Rebel Fleet, while Luke and R2–D2 make for Dagobah so that Luke can complete his Jedi training.

Yet, through all this, the Empire has not been idle. Darth Vader is supervising the construction of a new Death Star, far more powerful than the last. But the Imperial engineers are falling behind schedule and the Emperor himself arrives to fire a little extra enthusiasm into his workers. The Emperor is unconcerned by reports that the Rebels are massing for renewed hostilities. He has a foolproof plan for crushing the rebellion once and for all.

Meanwhile on Dagobah, Yoda and the ethereal form of Obi-wan Kenobi tell Luke that only by facing and killing his father, Darth Vader, can the influence of the Empire be extinguished once and for all. Luke is sure he cannot bring himself to kill his own flesh and blood. But Obi-wan has one more surprise. Leia is also the child of Darth Vader.

Elsewhere in the Galaxy, the Rebel forces, or rather what's left of them, are marshalling their ships in preparation for their final assault on the Empire. Lando Calrissian is to lead the fighter ship strike on the Empire's new Death Star orbiting the green moon of Endor, while Han, Chewie and Leia will sabotage the power station on the planet below, knocking out the uncompleted Death Star's force field. But before the operation begins, Luke arrives and is assigned to Han's assault force.

The four companions slip through the Imperial defences and, landing on Endor, hijack an Imperial patrol. In the ensuing battle, the friends split up and are captured by a fierce race of furry warriors called Ewoks. Reunited in the tree city of the Ewoks, Luke, Leia, Han and Chewie manage to convince the furry folk to join with them against the Empire. Then later, in the quiet of the evening, Luke reveals to Leia that they are brother and sister, then leaves to face their father alone at the Imperial base elsewhere on Endor.

Walking straight into Vader's trap, Luke tries to convince his father to betray the Emperor and join the Alliance. But Vader is too far gone. He confiscates his son's light-sabre and conducts Luke to the temporary throne room of the Emperor aboard the Death Star.

At that same moment, Han, Leia and Chewie are beginning their attack on the Endor power station. With the war-like Ewoks fighting on their side, the Rebels soon have the power station out of commission and Lando begins his attack run on the Death Star.

Back in the Emperor's throne room, Luke is battling with himself to resist the hypnotic powers of the Emperor. Regaining his light sabre, Luke engages Vader in hand-to-hand combat while the Emperor gloatingly looks on. But Luke's Jedi powers have grown over the months and after a savage battle Vader is downed. But Luke's troubles are far from over. The Emperor himself steps into the fray and renders Luke helpless with bolts of unimaginable power projected from his finger-tips. Luke is staring Death in the face and all seems lost until, with one final rally, Vader regains control of his true self and attacks his former master, hurling the Emperor to his doom at the nuclear heart of the Death Star. This final act redeems Vader and he dies a peaceful man, but not before urging his son to escape before the Rebel attack utterly destroys the Death Star. The Rebels' last stand is a magnificent success and that night his freedom fighters celebrate their victory and the return of liberty to the Galaxy with their Ewok allies on the planet of Endor. All plot threads are tied up. Han and Leia can finally indulge in their love for each other and Luke is finally at peace, knowing that his father repented his evil ways in time to enjoy an existence of a higher plane with his old friends Yoda and Obi-wan Kenobi.

FINDING MR WRITE

Originally, George Lucas had intended to tell the story of Luke Skywalker's struggle against the Empire in just one film. But as he completed the first draft of the tale, he realised that he had far too much story to fit into one two-hour movie. So he simply cut the story in two and continued to work on the first half. Before long it became apparent to Lucas that even two feature films would be too little screen time to tell the story in and three films would be needed.

Though Lucas wrote and directed *Star Wars: A New Hope*, the tremendous success of the film meant that Lucas's energies were divided between running Lucasfilm and overseeing the flood of merchandising

ABOVE: *Luke Skywalker (Mark Hamill) and Han Solo (Harrison Ford) discuss the disappearance of the Princess. (Lucasfilm Ltd).*

which followed in the Star wake, as well as overseeing preparations for future Lucasfilm movie projects. In short, there was no way Lucas could write or direct any more *Star Wars* films . . .even if he wanted to.

For *Empire Strikes Back*, Lucas had hired Lawrence Kasdan to craft the screenplay and Irvin Kershner to direct. With *Return of the Jedi*, he resolved to use a new writer/director team.

Yet, well-laid plans, particularly in the movie business, have a habit of going awry. The October 1981 issue of *Starlog* magazine carried a story under the title of *Kasdan Gets Revenge* (*Revenge of the Jedi* was the shooting title for *Return of the Jedi*).

'It's a big surprise to me that I'm writing *Revenge of the Jedi*,' said Kasdan. 'George Lucas called me on the phone and asked me to do the script as a favour to him. I told George that I hadn't planned on doing any more 'just writing' on films.' He said, "Aw, come on. I've done it. Paul Schrader did it for Martin Scorsese. What difference does it make?"

'I'm doing the script because I feel I owe George a lot. Besides, I like working with him. There's also a certain satisfaction in finishing the trilogy. Additionally, writing *Jedi* will be very rewarding financially.'

George Lucas had, as with *The Empire Strikes Back*, roughed out the plot of the movie first, embracing the main story-points and character developments. He was looking to Kasdan to bring pacing and humour to the final script. Kasdan, Lucas and the director, Richard Marquand, spent a solid week discussing the thrust of the story and settling any differences of opinion they had as to the direction *Return of the Jedi* should take. From there on it became Kasdan's baby.

'*Revenge of the Jedi*'s basic thrust is to wrap up the trilogy's story,' Kasdan revealed in the same interview. 'You can assume that *Jedi*'s structure will be like that of *Star Wars* and *Empire*, cutting back and forth. You could probably guess which of the characters will be returning. There will also be some new characters.'

Because of the suddenness of Lucas's request, Kasdan was left with little time in which to complete his assignment. 'It's a similar situation to the terrible time problem we had on *Empire*, but I think this time I'll have a much freer hand, because the *Jedi* screenplay George gave me isn't nearly as far along as *Empire*'s was.'

THE HAND ON THE HELM

The search for the man to direct *Jedi* was every bit as exhaustive as Lucas's original *Star Wars* casting sessions had been. Lucas started out with a list of literally hundreds of British and American directors who could, conceivably, direct the third part of the trilogy. After cutting away those who couldn't do the film because of scheduling, prior committments and lack of enthusiasm, the list fell to just two names, one of which was Richard Marquand whose previous credits included a horror movie called *The Legacy* and the war-time adventure movie *Eye of the Needle*.

'George Lucas told me he wanted a director who could work fast, somebody – possibly from television

OPPOSITE: *Han Solo (Harrison Ford) and the Princess (Carrie Fisher) are taken into custody by Imperial Forces.* BELOW: *Han Solo awakens from his carbon frozen sleep in* Return of the Jedi – *a by-product of the process is that he is temporarily blinded. (Lucasfilm Ltd).*

– who could think on his feet, improvise quickly, and work with actors. Finally – and I think this is the most important thing – somebody who could work with him,' said Richard Marquand. 'Finally, there were only two of us left in the running. This was about April or May of 1981.'

Though most people associated with *Return of the Jedi* have been reluctant to discuss who *didn't* get through the selection process, Mark Hamill did let it slip in an interview that Marquand's rival for the job was David Lynch, the young American director of *The Elephant Man*.

'David decided he didn't want to do a George Lucas movie,' explained Hamill, 'Because he felt he couldn't be constantly answering to another producer. George didn't want to restrict somebody that original, so they came to an amiable parting of the ways. Ironically, David left to make *Dune* for Dino de Laurentis.'

With Marquand selected to helm *Return of the Jedi*, preproduction work got under way with a vengeance. Marquand was far more than a puppet director, and had a healthy input into the way the movie would shape up as a kind of punch-line to the first two films.

'I had a whole plan of the way I wanted to present each character, each *new* character,' Marquand told me in February 1983, 'to make *Jedi* slightly different from the other films. *Empire* ends in a kind of explosion – everyone's going off in different directions. I thought it would be nice if we opened *Jedi* with a tremendous sense of mystery. A 'where is everybody?' sort of feeling. We know that Vader and the Emperor are really on the Rebel's tails after *Empire*, which ended on a kind of dark note. I thought it would be nice to pick up on that. All the heroes are scattered to the four corners of the Galaxy and then I could bring in each one in an interesting way. George liked that idea. Larry (Kasdan) picked up on it and turned it into something terrific. Then I was talking about killing off one of the main characters. George wouldn't have that.'

Richard Marquand's next step was to get together with the principal actors and hash out how the main characters would develop in the film.

'"You know this character. Tell me what this character's got to offer in terms of the public and the box-office and the story," I said. I discovered some nice things about the characters, which we were able to inject into the film.'

Marquand has nothing but praise for Hamill, Fisher, Ford, *et al*. 'Carrie Fisher has made no secret of the fact that she's this sort of boy in girl's clothing,' Marquand told me, 'who marches up and down and shouts at everybody. She felt her character could do with a bit of development. And that happened to coincide exactly with my feelings. In the last movie, the Princess became such a bitch, she really was a drag. I was sure there was a lot more depth there we could use. And more comedy, too. Turn her into more of a woman. So I worked with Carrie on that. She's a very sexy, attractive lady and in this film we'll get to find that out.

'Mark's character, Luke Skywalker, is the one that develops through the whole series. That's the area of jeopardy. Will Luke move towards the Dark Side of the Force? He does; you see the darkening as he is led in this direction.

'Billy Dee Williams had all sorts of ideas about Lando Calrissian. His past, and where he had come from, the kind of skills he had. We realise that he was the first owner of the Millennium Falcon. We didn't really get to know him in *Empire*, we just learned to distrust him.

'Harrison Ford's great, he really is. He's a very professional actor. A man who is now quite a major box office star. He gets on with it. Doesn't suffer fools gladly. If you don't know what you're going to do on the day, he gets a little confused and upset. But he's terrific as an ally, someone who understands the craft of being a movie actor.'

MAKING MOVIES

By January 11th, 1982, the *Return of the Jedi* cast and crew were safely ensconced in EMI's Elstree Studios just outside London, and shooting began. The production was using all nine sound-stages. Sets were put up and torn down with alarming speed as the juggernaut movie careened through its paces. Down came the gate of Jabba's Palace, up went the Death Star docking bay. *Jedi* technicians built an impressive redwood forest inside one hangar-like sound stage, then built the Ewok village among the trees.

Studio shooting forged ahead at break-neck speed and was completed in an amazing 78 days. From there, Marquand and his team flew to America and spent the next eight weeks filming the Tatooine scenes in the blazing heat of the Arizona desert. The Endor scenes were shot in the cooler redwood forests of Northern California.

In an effort to keep the curious at bay, and the prices of the local shop-keepers down, the Arizona filming was conducted under a cover title of *Blue Harvest* – 'Horror Beyond Imagination' said the crew's tee-shirts. 'Is that what the film's about?' asked somebody of George Lucas, 'No,' he replied wryly, 'that's the making of the movie.'

Marquand explained his directing technique to the American magazine *Prevue* in an interview published just before the release of *Jedi*. He admitted that he rehearsed the actors, 'but *not* in their moves. I like to show them the sets, give them an idea of the action and go through the script with them very carefully. I can't stand it when an actor walks on the set saying he cannot deliver a line that a writer, a producer and a director spent eight months working on. I won't have it.'

Yet Harrison Ford is well-known in movie circles for the amount of input he likes to have into the script. Marquand was aware of this preference and had no criticism of Ford in this area. If Ford wanted dialogue changes, Marquand was prepared to accommodate him because, 'he'll have good reasons and he'll say it a week before shooting. He'll explain why, and you'll either agree, in which case you'll go to the producer and the other actors and express his points, or you'll explain why the line is there. If you can explain it to him, he'll do it because he's a professional.'

Overall, Marquand's aim was to create 'real relationships and real action that stem from real emotions.' He was wary, rightly so, of allowing the dazzling special effects to take control of the film. But if he needed help, he felt secure in the knowledge that George Lucas would always be on hand to help him out.

'Having George Lucas as an executive producer on this film is like directing *King Lear* with Shakespeare in the next room!' said Marquand.

Lucas himself had sufficient confidence in his *Star Wars* movies to put his money where his mouth is. Unlike other major movie productions, which borrow money from wherever they can get it, then insure their borrowings like crazy in case the film flops, Lucas was using his personal fortune to finance *Jedi*.

'I decided,' said Lucas, 'I had the most faith in my own films. I'm using my profits to make more films.'

And Lucas's secret was to incorporate into his movies something that most contemporary film-makers forget. 'One of the most important things is to create an emotion in the audience,' says Lucas. 'The movie can be funny, sad or scary, but there *has* to be an emotion. It has to make you feel good or laugh or jump out of your seat.' Whether Lucas had injected enough emotion into *Jedi* would be left to the critics, and more importantly, the audiences to decide.

RELEASE OF THE JEDI

It's unlikely that George Lucas was really worried that *Jedi* would turn out to be a clinker. The film opened on the traditional date of May 25th, 1983 in America, followed by the British release on June 2nd, 1983. Although the reviews were, in the main, favourable, a few harder-to-please folk managed to find fault with the film. 'Taken on its own terms,' ventured *Time* magazine, '*Return of the Jedi* is a brilliant, imaginative piece of film-making.' *Time* then went on to say that *Jedi* sacrificed the human element for its fascination with dazzling special effects, a familiar complaint of the 'up-market' magazines of the *Star Wars* films. 'The other flaw,' said *Time*, 'is the ending: in all three films, Lucas has almost entirely avoided the rank sentimentality to which his story is vulnerable. In the final minutes of *Jedi*, he succumbs, however, and ends his trilogy with one of the corniest conclusions in recent years.'

Playboy's Bruce Williamson thought that *Jedi* was, 'another rousing entertainment in George Lucas's nine-part epic derived from *Star Wars*. . . in its script, *Return of the Jedi* falls a bit short of its predecessors and director Richard Marquand doesn't quite have Lucas's magic touch. . . Lucas continues to make movie-going the kind of innocent, awe-struck pleasure it used to be when we were all light-years younger.'

Variety, the trade paper of American show business, seemed to fall into line with the criticisms that *Time* had made. 'Lucas and Co have perfected the technical magic where anything and everything – no matter how bizarre – is believable. . . the human and dramatic dimensions have been sorely sacrificed. . . Harrison Ford, who was such an essential element of the first two outings is present more in body than in spirit this time, given little to do but react to special effects.'

Audiences either didn't read the reviews, or didn't care what they said anyway. The film was safely into profit inside three months and, as the end of 1983 rolled round, *Jedi* was the number three film among the top box-office grossers of all time.

BELOW: *Han Solo (Harrison Ford) creeps furtively around the Imperial power plant on the Planet Endor. (Lucasfild Ltd).*

ABOVE: *Han Solo (Harrison Ford) and Princess Leia (Carrie Fisher) on the planet of Endor. (Lucasfilm Ltd).*

Harrison Ford was not surprised that George Lucas had been proved right again and that most of the critics were out of touch with what the audiences wanted. 'People want fairy tales in their lives,' he told *Time* magazine. 'I'm lucky enough to provide them. There is no difference between doing this kind of film and playing *King Lear*. The actor's job is exactly the same: dress up and pretend.'

Ford had only one clash of opinion with the film-makers on *Jedi*. 'I thought it would give the myth some body (if Han Solo were to be killed off). Solo really had no place to go. He's got no papa, he's got no mama, he's got no story. But that was the one thing I was unable to convince George of.'

THE LAST ACT OF HAN SOLO

Return of the Jedi marked the final film in the middle trilogy of the *Star Wars* saga. It also marked the last screen appearances of Luke Skywalker, Princess Leia and Han Solo. Other stories in the epic tale would tell of the Clone Wars and the rise of the Empire in the first trilogy and rebuilding of the Galactic Democracy in the final trio of movies. Harrison Ford was not entirely unhappy that his stint as an interstellar star was over. 'The story that Han Solo was part of,' explained Ford to *Starburst's* Tony Crawley, 'which is *The Adventures of Luke Skywalker* in my guise of best friend is over. The story completes itself in this third film. I had a great time on *Jedi*. I'm glad I did it. I'm glad I did all three of them. But as

well, I'm glad. . . I don't. . . have to do any more. After *Jedi*, the saga goes back in time, so Solo's not in the next three. There will be nine films in all. Just three for Solo. I assume they will not replace me with another person to play Solo. . .'

INDIANA JONES AND THE TEMPLE OF. . . WHAT?

With such *Raiders of the Lost Ark* ripoffs as *Treasure of the Four Crowns* and *High Road to China* (ironically starring Lucas' first choice for Indiana Jones, Tom Selleck) thick on the ground, it came as no surprise when Lucasfilm announced a sequel. The news broke in the April 23rd, 1983 edition of the British movie trade paper, *Screen International*, with little fanfare. The 'In Production' section merely gave a detailed listing of the entire crew and the film's two stars, Harrison Ford and Kate Capshaw.

The American screen trade paper, *Variety*, was equally terse in its coverage of the story. 'Steven Spielberg is helming *Indiana Jones and the Temple of Doom* on location in Sri Lanka (with lensing in Hong Kong and London's Elstree Studios to follow) for Lucasfilm Ltd and Paramount, with Harrison Ford reprising his title role characterisation first seen in *Raiders of the Lost Ark* and Douglas Slocombe back as cinematographer. Kate Capshaw, who had roles in *A Little Sex* and the current sci-fier *Dreamscape* is Ford's new leading lady.' All of which was probably something of a surprise to certain American fan magazines which were getting excited about a new *Raiders* film called *Indiana Jones and the Temple of Death*.

Other than that, information was hard to come by. Nobody was talking, least of all Harrison Ford. Not that Ford would have put talking to the Press very high on his list of priorities anyway. He had married Melissa Mathison on March 14th, 1983, a short time after obtaining his final divorce from Mary and mere weeks before beginning work on *Indiana Jones*.

What was known is that Lawrence Kasdan, busy with directing his latest film, *The Big Chill*, had passed on the scripting chores. Lucas had turned to his old friends Gloria Katz and Willard Huyck, who had worked wonders with Lucas's original draft of *American Graffiti*.

Lucas himself had hinted at the contents of the four remaining *Indiana Jones* films around the time *Raiders of the Lost Ark* was released and confessed that Indy was probably his own favourite character. 'If I could be a dream figure, I'd be Indy,' he told American magazine *Rolling Stone*. 'It's not just that I'm interested in archeology or anthropology; a lot of that got into *Star Wars*, too. It's just that Indy can do anything. He's like a lot of Thirties heroes put together. He's this renegade archeologist and adventurer, but he's also a college professor, and he's got this Cary Grant side, too. In some stories, we'll see him in top hat and tails. We don't want to make him Superman – he's just open to all possibilities. *Raiders* will be the most action-oriented of the Indiana Jones movies – the others should deal more with the Occult.'

Lucas had no problems convincing director Steven Spielberg to re-sign on the dotted line. 'I'd hate to let it slip through my fingers into somebody else's hands,' said Spielberg. 'I'll certainly not be involved in the third or fourth one, but I really want to do the follow-up, because the story is even more spectacular than *Raiders*.'

As it happens, Spielberg announced in the early part of 1984 that he *would* be directing the third Raiders film, should it happen, and Ford too had been signed for the project.

Meanwhile, Harrison Ford was expressing his pleasure at the prospect of appearing in *Indiana Jones and the Temple of Doom*. 'Of *course* I'm doing the second *Raiders* film,' he told *Starburst* magazine. 'With great pleasure. We begin in 1983 and for the first time, I think, in the history of sequels and good directors, Steven (Spielberg) is going to direct it. So this is very exciting for me. It was one of the best working relationship experiences of my life working with Steven.'

Pleased as he was, Ford was a little disturbed to hear, from *Starburst's* Tony Crawley, that there were a total of five Indiana Jones films on the Lucasfilm launching pad, in varying stages of development. After completing filming on *Return of the Jedi*, the actor said, 'Actually, I'm only committed to one film at the moment. That's another Indiana Jones film. I had hoped to have a year off between the end of *Jedi* and the beginning of the next Indy film. (Five Indiana Jones films) is okay with me. I mean I really enjoy working on them. And I really enjoy the character very much. And certainly I couldn't hope for any better company than Lucas and Spielberg. But having done one, I don't think I'd do four more of anything. They must be talking to Roger Moore. . . one at a time for me!'

Filming on *Indiana Jones* proceeded almost without incident until, near the end of the schedule in September 1983, Ford fell from an elephant and injured his back. The production was shuttered for two weeks while Ford was flown back to the States for emergency laser therapy. Despite some speculation in the trade press, Ford made a full recovery and happily, the movie was completed in time for the scheduled opening date of May 25th, 1984 in American cinemas, though the British premiere would have to wait until June 6th.

CHAPTER 8

HARRISON FORD: THINKING ACTOR

Carpenter, Actor, Common Man, Sage

'What's so attractive about Harrison Ford is that you wouldn't recognise him on the street. You wouldn't know him in a crowd, you might not even know him at a small cocktail party of a dozen people. He really is a chameleon. When he's acting, he becomes the character he's playing, and afterwards he reverts to being Harrison Ford, wood-cutter and furniture maker. His magic is that he's a very accessible, common guy.'

Steven Spielberg, director of *Indiana Jones and the Temple of Doom*

Harrison Ford has been around the movie acting business for more than fifteen years. From his first film, *Dead Heat on a Merry-Go-Round* (1967), to his most recent, *Indiana Jones and the Temple of Doom* (1984), his attitudes to fame, wealth and success have remained surprisingly consistent. He is proof, if proof were ever needed, that becoming a big-time movie star needn't change one's life for the worse. He has displayed an admirable ability to keep the craziness of Hollywood and film-making in general firmly in perspective.

He isn't over-awed with his own on-screen image and can always be counted on for a breath of common sense in an all-too-looney business.

'My mission when I started in the business,' he smiles, 'was simply not to have to do anything else for a living. And now, my only mission is to do good work. For me, that depends on the idea, the script. I can't foresee what will come up in the future, so I can't have focused ambition. I have a lot of carpentry projects. I know that much. I design all the things I make at home. I used to be much more involved with carpentry. I just don't have the time any more to put hand to hammer.'

Ford is too level-headed a person to let media name-tags like 'Star' bother him too much. 'I don't consider myself to be a star,' he told *Starburst* magazine shortly after the release of *Star Wars*. 'I'm much too aware of the functionality of that word. I don't happen to think I'm good enough. I'm a perfectionist and I always think I could have done things better. That's one reason why I never see

rushes of any film I am making. I never know how the character is going to work out. I never really know, not even when I eventually see the final movie. Because I can't stand to see myself. I know how much better it might have been if I'd had the intelligence at the time – that's the worst part about filming, absolutely the worst part. Now, I just want to keep on working. You grow older and your career changes. All the better. I just hope things are still as scary as they are now for my next seven years. Well, not scary – but needing to keep on your toes. I'd like to be surprised at the parts offered me. I'd like roles that I'd never imagined for myself. If you start churning out bull, it lives on long after you've flushed yourself. It's still up there, 40ft high and 60ft wide screaming, "Bull! Bull! This guy was a fraud."'

Wary as Ford may have been about the term star, there's no arguing that *Star Wars* made him a media personality. With just about every person in the civilised world having seen the film, he had to cope with the fact that he was recognised in public as being Han Solo.

'Under certain circumstances, if I'm where people expect to see that sort of person – or whatever they think that sort of person is like – then I'm generally more recognisable than if I'm someplace ordinary people congregate, which is the place I'm more likely to be. But a lot of people recognise me, and some of them say something about it, and some of them don't. But I'm aware when I'm pegged. Basically, I don't like it, because it takes me out of my favourite position, which is the unseen observer. It puts me in a

BELOW: *Indiana Jones (Harrison Ford) and his old enemy Belloq (Paul Freeman) meet in a Cairo bar in* Raiders of the Lost Ark, *(Lucasfilm Ltd)*. OPPOSITE: *Harrison Ford as Mike Barnsby in* Force Ten From Navarone. *(AIP)*.

RLA-6179

position of being observed, which has no profitability whatsoever. I generally have no problem with the people who approach me. But often they don't know who the hell I am, or they don't care. Sometimes they think my name is Han Solo, and sometimes they don't know what my name is. Some know quite well what my name is and all about the movies I've been in. And when I'm asked to sign an autograph, I'll sign it – if I'm not having sex at the time or doing something important. I don't have any trouble dealing with people. People are generally very kind. It may change.'

As well as being spotted on the streets by *Star Wars* fans, Ford noticed that suddenly he had fan mail. But rather than allowing himself to be buried in a deluge of letters asking for anything from an autograph to a piece of clothing, Ford passed the chore on. 'I get my mail dealt with by the studios, but there are times when you look out the window and see a pair of eyes peering back at you through the bushes.'

In fact, Ford is far more interested in being an actor than a star. 'At this point in my career,' he said at the time of *Raiders'* release, 'I'd like to do more contrasting roles. My attitude is a reflection of my early TV experiences, and a lack of a formal theatrical discipline. I just don't have the patience to do methodical, safe, repetitious formula acting. I like film acting because every experience is new – new sets, new actors, new directors. The stage is a confining medium where everything is too calculated.

'I also prefer film because I have such a poor memory. What I do – my method if you will – is to convince myself to believe in the reality of a situation. The Let's Pretend School of Acting.

'Actually, my approach calls upon my survival skills the same way boy scouts leave kids alone in the woods with two matches and a pocket knife. You get a scenario of action, some words, and you are expected to travel between two points in a believable manner. What goes on in my mind is so personal and above explanation that it's torturous to reveal.

'Of course, I have technical tricks and fundamental skills, but they were largely self-taught, because I was such a bad learner. I profit from experience. I think acting classes teach you how to act in acting classes. I've made an awful fool of myself on film a number of times as a result, but that's how I learn.

'I do know my limitations, though. If I ever found myself thinking, "I could do *Streetcar* better than Brando," I'd wash my mind out with soap. I am simply happy to be working. Film acting is an honest, professional activity and an experience that I enjoy. I only ever wanted to make a decent living out of it.

'I must admit that I've been extremely lucky. That's an oft-repeated homily, but true. My success is more accident than accomplishment.'

Yet Ford is careful to distinguish between believing in the characters he is portraying and losing himself in them. 'I don't live out my fantasies,' he said in 1981, 'I choose from amongst what is offered to me at any given time. I look for parts that contrast with the last thing I've done. I don't wish to do the same thing twice, and I try to put as much distance between past characters as possible. The reason I choose something depends on a lot of things. Whether I like the people involved and think I can get along properly with them. Whether I think it's good and worthwhile to do. A lot of different elements enter into it. . . whether I want to work at that time.'

The creating of a character is one of the things that will draw Ford to one project or another. 'I have very particular feelings about the characters I play, but my way of articulating them is through the medium of film, not in 25 words or less. I couldn't do that for

BELOW: *An early publicity photograph of Harrison Ford from his days as a contract player.*

myself. I grow a character, rather than delineate him from the word 'go'. I'm more interested in making a character up out of the story parts. I prefer to work that way than to impose a character as a whole piece onto the film to start with, although it's sometimes necessary to do that. And I try to put as much of myself into the characters as possible – not my recognisable self – but my mind is always there. I don't know how you could not put elements of yourself into a part – or why it would be profitable to keep those elements out. It's the unique thing about a person – any person – which makes him or her interesting.'

Ford likes to think of acting as a kind of logical progressive process – more a craft than an art – and is fond of comparing it to carpentry. 'Both are crafts,' he told *The Times*. 'I taught myself acting the same way I taught myself carpentry. You submit yourself to the logic of the craft. My approach to both jobs is almost entirely technical. What I learnt from carpentry, above all, was the work ethic. I used to be very lazy, but now I find I can't enjoy myself when I'm not working. It's allied to my problem of not being able to distract myself when I'm waiting around on a film set. Those big films, like *Star Wars* and *Raiders*, are technically very complex, so that the actors have to wait a long time between takes. I sit and stare at the walls or I walk around and bump into the front and the back of my trailer. Either I'm thinking about the next scene or I'm in a state of mental suspension. I can't read or concentrate on anything else. It's the worst thing about being an actor, for me.'

As well as waiting around for the floor crews to prepare the physical effects on movie, you'd think Ford would be pretty tired of reacting to blank blue screens, where the film-makers will later drop in the special effects scenes of space ships battling one another or hideous creatures closing in for the kill. Not Ford.

'I wish I could take everyone with me on a film so they could get a clear idea of what the process of film-making is like, really, in practical terms. Special effects include miniatures, which are done in the post-production phase; matte shots, in which part of what you see on the screen is live-action, includes actors, with some background matted in; mechanical effects, such as craft going up on wires. All of these things have *nothing* to do with the acting process. The supposed difficulty of acting with special effects does not exist. It's not difficult to imagine that if this room was a set, I'm seeing the approach of a dozen star cruisers coming towards us, or to imagine, if this was a set, there were an ocean and tennis courts out there, any more than there would be a dozen star ships. So what is the difference? It's exactly the same.'

None of which is to say that there are *no* problems attached to working within the constraints of special effects. 'If we were matting in starships outside this window, I'd be obliged not to move past the frame on this side or that side of the window. But I'm getting money for that. That's no problem. Special effects are no more difficult than having to work with another person. If you and I were in a scene, and you were lit from back there, I'd be obliged not to move from here. It might be necessary for me to be here for the framing. If I moved to there, they'd have to cut (Ford indicates 'here' to 'there' with the slightest inclination of the head). That's the kind of constraint you're under. I quite enjoy dealing with all the technical problems. If I were obliged not to move

LEFT: *Han Solo (Harrison Ford) rushes Princess Leia (Carrie Fisher) to safety through the tunnels beneath* The Empire Strikes Back's *Ice Planet of Hoth. (Lucasfilm Ltd).*

from here to there, I'd be able to find a source of inspiration. When it came time for my close-up, I'd be rivetted here for some reason. Either I would stare at you in a way that would prohibit my moving or something else. But it's always weaving the bits together to make something as real as possible.'

One very real problem attached to films which contain a dazzling array of special effects is that they are received with varying degrees of suspicion by both critics and the Hollywood establishment. The film industry has, without marked success, tried to imitate the Lucas style of movie making by creating special effects extravaganzas at the cost of the stories and the characters. The critics seem to have laid the blame for this explosion unfairly and squarely at the door of George Lucas, dubbing his films 'comic book movies', an accusation which Ford doesn't take kindly to.

'In Europe, I think films tend to be more like literature. The concerns are literary. In America, we have evolved a film which is, perhaps, different. And I feel there is as much opportunity for expression and action in a scene without dialogue as in a scene with. So I don't see that similarity with comic books. Because it's not literature doesn't mean it's a comic book for me. And I think that's the extension that's being made. If it's not full of serious, metaphysical concerns, then it must be a comic book.

'I'm aware that there are very complicated ideas in some comic books, but this kind of comment does not seem to apply, but a number of times I've heard this said. . . that the characters are less real than they might be in other circumstances.

'I work hard to avoid making a character too simple. I think in *Raiders of the Lost Ark*, the screenwriters, the people who created the concept of the character, did me a great service as an actor by providing me with a strong opening scene in which you *think* you know everything about the character, and then you get a hard cut to the same person under circumstances you would never have anticipated. Now this produces anything but a two-dimensional character, *I* think. But I suppose I should leave that judgement to other people.

'I see my films as *films*. I see the characters as

expressive, as full as the film has time. I don't see a limitation on the experience that 'a film being like a comic book' suggests to me. If a film *is* like a comic book, then to me, it's not enough like a film.

'And the other criticism – while we're at it! – is how do you feel being upstaged by special effects, being in a film where the characters are totally unimportant compared to the special effects. And I usually say to that comment: Who's at fault here? We're talking about awfully good directors here. I don't think they do that. If they do – where is the audience during this period of time? They've no emotional touchstone on the screen. They're just sitting there watching trucks collide with no people in them. That's not interesting. *Nobody* would be interested in that situation.

'But I think this also proceeds from a cultural difference between what film has *come* to mean in Europe and in America. . .

'I for one feel that intellectual concerns are probably better dealt with in books. There's more depth of potential for intellectual definition in a book than, maybe, in a film. Although there's more chance for empathy, more chance for emotional contact in a film than in a book.

'I also think there is a kind of idea in Europe, and among European critics, that entertainment is less than salutary. Entertainment is something we should look down our noses at.

'This, I think, is very wrong. We, in America, have gone through a cycle of films that were full of social commentary and social relevance. What happened in America is that all the socially relevant film did was

co-opt the problem. They spoke about a problem and then they presented a solution that was really a movie solution. Not a real solution for the real world. It was imposed by the mechanism, by the necessity to be, to a certain degree, commercially successful.'

THE HALLMARKS OF SUCCESS

As with any other person in the movie business who has rocketed, in this case quite literally, to success, Harrison Ford has to contend with people who want to hitch their wagon to the tail of his comet. One of the ways in which this trend is most apparent is in the number of unsolicited scripts that cascade through the post with his name on the wrapper.

'By and large, every time I'm in a successful film, I receive a whole bunch of material, imitations from people looking to get the same job done, and I don't read those. Then there's another level of stuff that comes in and I simply do not agree with the intentions of what those people are after. That's the second biggest body of rejections. And then if I can find something with an idea I can live with and if the character is not the same as I've played last time, then I will begin to consider who's involved and when it's going to happen. About twenty a week come into the office. They send them to my business manager as well as my agent. My car mechanic gets a stack, too! The only point of departure is the last thing I've done. I have been associated with a lot of successful

BELOW: *Rick Deckard stalks his inhuman prey through the teeming streets of Los Angeles in* Blade Runner. *(Ladd Co).* OPPOSITE: *Harrison Ford off duty.*

entertainment. I don't necessarily want to be taken seriously, but I would like to do some serious roles. Unfortunately one must be thought of as serious before one is offered serious roles.'

But for Ford, the most important thing when considering a new acting role is not to have his judgement swayed by the financial rewards attached to the job. 'Never do it for the money,' he says. 'That's the biggest lesson. The potential for embarrassment and humiliation is much too great to do it for the money. But now I can decide not to do it for the money. As an aesthetic principle. It's what made the difference between being able to work and not being able to work. When I was doing television, I wasn't making a living as an actor. I was working ten times a year. But I wasn't making a decent living and I had no prospects. I wasn't learning anything about what I was doing. I wasn't appearing in anything that had enough quality in it to enable me to live up to my potential, or go beyond it. So I quit being an actor, not because I didn't want to be an actor, but because I didn't want to make money doing that bull over and over again. I thought I would wear out my face and wear out my welcome and I would never get another chance at the kind of stuff I wanted to do. So for eight years I did carpentry and appeared in three or four movies, all good ones. So I was then beginning to be associated with good work.'

When quizzed over whether it is difficult to cope with the pressures financial and career success has brought, Ford answers a little dismissively. 'I was never level-headed before, so it hasn't been an enormous change in my life. There's an enormous change in the freedom. Money for me is just an enormous amount of freedom, and I enjoy it. I was poor for a long, long time and now I don't have any problem with making money.

'And how could success bother me? I struggled for so long, and I always saw other actors, younger than me, making it big. I wondered if it would ever be my turn. But life is like that, sometimes. I believe if you wait long enough, you'll get your reward. Or just deserts, as the case may be. I've done work I'm proud of, like in Coppola's films *The Conversation* and *Apocalypse Now*. Those are very highly regarded, and when I'm famous enough, maybe people will look back and say, "gee, I didn't know he was a good actor, too." I've done comedy, romance, you name it. But it's the teens, the kids, who have given me this success. They're the ones who not only saw me as Han and Indy, but they kept going back, making those films the biggest hits of all time.

'It is today that counts, not what was yesterday or will be tomorrow. Fifteen years ago when I was starting, I could not have handled this degree of success. I am a late bloomer. I resisted maturity because I had to learn my job and that takes a long time. In a way, I still resist maturity. I like to play – fortunately my work is my pleasure.'

Nevertheless, all this success did have a negative side effect on Ford's life. It coincided with the breakdown of his marriage of fifteen years to his college sweetheart, Mary, the mother of his two sons. 'We simply grew apart and, although she has custody of our two sons, we've remained as amicable as possible in the circumstances. They don't live too far away from me and I see the boys regularly, which is great. They're pretty well adjusted and seem to be taking my success in their stride.

'I probably wasn't easy to be married to. I respond to a sort of barometric presssure and this is a stressful occupation. In the dark spaces of my personality I show it. I can be moody. I am independent, but not solitary. I like people in ones and twos, not parties. I'm a very ordinary person whose fear is being stuck in a typical Hollywood party for an eternity. If I die and don't go to Heaven, you just might find me in purgatory in a disco.'

HARRISON FORD = BOX OFFICE?

Harrison Ford's success is almost at that height where the mere mention of his name in connection with a movie – any movie – is almost enough to guarantee a profit. Such a thought alarms Ford. 'But I don't expect every film I make to be a box-office success, period. This is something that never even occurs to me. As often as it's happened, how could you anticipate that it would happen again? My luck is enormous.

'But my skills at seeing into the future are really not as great as my luck. Also I'm not looking for commercial viability. I'm lucky enough to have had enough success that I feel I can deal with a certain number of films that are not going to be big, commercial successes.

'Every film you make has to have its potential to make its money back and make a fair enough profit, so that people won't feel they've wasted their time.

So, yes, I want that. But I'd also like to make films for a smaller segment of the audience. You just don't take the demographics then make up a script that reflects the concerns of the broadest number of people. You work in another way – from the other direction.'

With all this acting success it seems a little surprising that Harrison Ford hasn't gone the way of other successful stars and set up his own production company, to develop pet projects for himself, nor has he gone the directing route.

'So far I haven't been able to figure out a way of becoming involved in a process like that. One of the major problems in developing a property for yourself, or having something developed for you, is that it tends to be made *for you*. And who you are is what you want to change.

'I would prefer to come to something that has a strength of its own, a life of its own, and then add something to that. If I feel somebody makes something for me, they're going to use what they think are my strengths. Maybe they'll try to stretch me a little bit. But they'll always have me in mind. I want them to have a character in mind. Then I want to come in at the last minute.

'I don't even want to hear that somebody has written something with me in mind.'

And directing? 'I simply have no ambitions in that area. That job involves too much planning and preparation. I'm more of an on-the-spot, spontaneous individual. Frankly I have no long-term goals. I'm just getting used to the idea of not having to worry about money any more. Actors who want to turn director are a pain. It's just enough to research a part, period, and go out there and do it. My advice to other actors? Rely on experience and intuition, get a good night's sleep. Who wants to be a director?'

ACKNOWLEDGEMENTS

No book is ever a solo effort. My main collaborators in this biography were Harrison Ford (of course) through his quotes in the many interviews he has given in the years since *Star Wars* shot him to international fame, my *Starburst* colleague Tony Crawley who made available to me the notes from the several interviews he has conducted with Harrison Ford, Francesca Landau who did the bulk of the research at a time when the deadline seemed to be pressing in, and Phil Edwards who read through the manuscript and gave many helpful suggestions as to where the book could be improved. And a special tip of the hat to John Reeves of *Video Screen*, Chelmsford who helped out with information on video releases of Ford Films.

I also have to thank my Zomba colleagues, Publisher Maxim Jakubowski who agreed on the spot to the project, Editor Emily White who had the almost thankless task of trying to make sense of my manuscript, and Steve O'Leary who designed the book you are now holding in your hands.

During the course of researching this project, I read or quoted from a whole host of writers: Ralph Appelbaum, Alan Arnold, David Badder, Hilary Bonner, John Brosnan, Ken Bruzenak, Vic Bulluck, James H.Burns, Mike Bygrave, Gerald Clarke, Minty Clinch, Richard Combs, Phil Edwards, Dave Farrow, Clinton Gilmore, Joan Goodman, Marianne Gray, Robert Greenburger, George Haddad-Garcia, Alex Harvey, Clive Hirchhorn, Ann Holler, David Houston, Saul Kahan, David Lewin, Herb A.Lightman, David Litchfield, Iain F.McAsh, Milo Mitchell, Peter Noble, Kerry O'Quinn, Richard Patterson, David Pirie, Dale Pollock, Tony Pratt, Alasdair Riley, Tim Satchell, Norman Spinrad, Michael Sragow, Philip Strick, Peter Sullivan, James Van Hise, Jo Weedon, Bruce Williamson, and David Wilson. Their interviews and features appeared in *American Cinematographer, The Blade Runner Souvenir Magazine, cinema, City Limits, Daily Mail, Daily Mirror, Films Illustrated, A Journal of the Making of the Empire Strikes Back, Mail on Sunday, Monthly Film Bulletin, Movie Guide, Movie Star, Ms London, Photoplay, Playboy, Prevue, Raiders of the Lost Ark Collectors' Album, Ritz, Rolling Stone, Screen International, Skywalking, Starburst, Starlog, The Sun, Sunday, Time, Time Out, The Times,* and *Woman's Own.*

Into all this I folded in interviews conducted in collaboration with Phil Edwards with many of Ford's co-workers, including Anthony Daniels, Carrie Fisher, Richard Marquand, Syd Mead, Ivor Powell, and Ridley Scott.

All pictures are copyright the production companies noted in the captions and were supplied by the production companies, The Phil Edwards Fantasy Film Archive, Alan McKenzie Collection and the Steve O'Leary Collection.

If I've left anyone out, abject apologies and my thanks, too.

Alan McKenzie

Dead Heat on a Merry-Go-Round (1966)

Starring James Coburn (*Eli Kotch*), Camilla Sparv (*Inger Knudson*), Aldo Ray (*Eddie Hart*), Nina Wayne (*Frieda Schmid*), Robert Webber (*Milo Stewart*), Rose Marie (*Margaret Kirby*), Todd Armstrong (*Alfred Morgan*), Marian Moses (*Dr Marion Hague*), Michael Strong (*Paul Feng*), Severn Darden (*Miles Fisher*), James Westerfield (*Jack Balter*), Philip E.Pine (*George Logan*), Simon Scott (*William Anderson*), Ben Astar (*General Mailenkoff*), Lawrence Mann (*Officer Howard*), Michael St.Angel (*Captain William Yates*), Alex Rodine (*Translator*), Albert Nalbandian (*Willie Manus*), Tyler McVey (*Lyman Mann*), Roy Glenn (*Sergeant Elmer K.Coxe*), Harrison Ford (*Bellboy*).
Directed by Bernard Girard, Screenplay by Bernard Girard, Photographed by Lionel Linden, Edited by William Lyon, Art direction by Walter M.Simonds, Music by Stu Phillips, Produced by Carter DeHaven, Production Company DeHaven-Girard for Columbia, Time: 107 mins.

Luv (1967)

Starring Jack Lemmon (*Harry Berlin*), Peter Falk (*Milt Manville*), Elaine May (*Ellen*), Nina Wayne (*Linda*), Eddie Mayehoff (*Attorney Goodhart*), Paul Martman (*Doyle*), Severn Darden (*Vandergrist*), and Harrison Ford.
Directed by Clive Donner, Screenplay by Elliott Baker, based on the play by Murray Schisgal, Photographed by Ernest Laszlo, Produced by Martin Manulis, Production Company Jalem, Time: 96 mins.

The Long Ride Home (1967, aka: A Time for Killing)

Starring Glenn Ford (*Major Walcott*), George Hamilton (*Captain Bentley*), Inger Stevens (*Emily Biddle*), Paul Petersen (*Blue Lake*), Max Baer (*Sgt Luther Liskell*), Todd Armstrong (*Lt Prudessing*), Timothy Carey (*Billy Cat*), Kenneth Toby (*Sgt Cleehan*), Richard X.Slattery (*Corp Paddy Darling*), Duke Hobbie (*Lt Frist*), Dean Stanton (*Sgt Dan Way*), James Davidson (*Little Mo*), Harrison J.Ford (*Lt Shaffer*), Charlie Briggs (*Sgt Kettlinger*), Kay E. Kuter (*Owelson*), Dick Miller (*Zollic officer*), Craig Curtis (*Bagnef*), Emile Miller (*Col Harries*), Marshall Reed (*Stedner*), Jay Ripley (*Lovingwood*), Dean Goodhill (*Bruce*).
Directed by Phil Carlson, Screenplay by Halsted Welles, based on the novel *Southern Blade* by Nelson and Shirley Wolford, Photographed by Kenneth Peach, Edited by Roy Livingston, Music by Mundell Lowe, Produced by Harry Joe Brown, Production Company Columbia/Sage Western Pictures, Time: 83 mins.

Journey to Shiloh (1967)

Starring James Caan (*Buck Burnett*), Michael Sarrazin (*Miller Nalls*), Brenda Scott (*Gabrielle Du Prey*), Don Stroud (*Todo McLean*), Paul Petersen (*J.C.Sutton*), Michael Burns (*Eubie Bell*), Michael Vincent (*Little Bit Buck*), Harrison Ford (*Willie Bill Beardon*), John Doucette (*Gen Braxton Bragg*).
Directed by William Hale, Screenplay by Gene Coon, based on the novel *Fields of Honour* by Will Henry, Photographed by Enzo A.Martinelli, Produced by Howard Christie, Production Company Universal Pictures, Time: 81 mins.

Getting Straight (1970)

Starring Elliott Gould (*Harry Bailey*), Candice Bergen (*Jan*), Robert F.Lyons (*Nick*), Jeff Corey (*Dr Wilhunt*), Max Julien (*Ellis*), Cecil Kellaway (*Dr Kasper*), John Lormer (*Vandenburg*), Leonard Stone (*Lysander*), William Bramley (*Wade Linden*), Jeannie Berlin (*Judy Kramer*), John Rubenstein (*Herbert*), Richard Anders (*Dr Greengrass*), Brenda Sykes (*Luan*), Jenny Sullivan (*Sheila*), Gregory Sierra (*Garcia*), Billie Bird (*Landlady*), Harrison Ford (*Jake*), Elizabeth Lane (*Alice Linden*), Hilarie Thompson (*Cynthia*), Irene Tedrow (*Mrs Stebbins*), Joanna Serpe (*Room-mate*), Scott Perry (*Airline Representative*).
Directed by Richard Rush, Screenplay by Robert Kaufman, based on the novel by Ken Kolb, Photographed by Lazlo Kovacs, Edited by Maury Winetrobe, Produced by Richard Rush, Production Company The Organisation, Time: 125 mins.

American Graffiti (1973)

Starring Richard Dreyfuss (*Curt*), Ron Howard (*Steve*), Paul Le Mat (*John*), Charles Martin Smith (*Terry the Toad*), Cindy Williams (*Laurie*), Candy Clark (*Debbie*), Mackenzie Phillips (*Carol*), Wolfman Jack (*Disc Jockey*), Harrison Ford (*Bob Falfa*), Bo Hopkins (*Joe*), Manuel Padilla (*Carlos*), Beau Gentry (*Ants*), Kathleen Quinlan (*Peg*), Suzanne Somers (*Blonde in T-Bird*), Debralee Scott (*Falfa's Girl*).
Directed by George Lucas, Screenplay by George Lucas, Gloria Katz and Willard Huyck, Photographed by Haskell Wexler, Ron Eveslage and Jan Dalquen, Edited by Verna Fields and Marcia Lucas, Sound and recording by Walter Murch, Casting by Fred Roos and Mike Fenton, Co-produced by Gary Kurtz, Produced by Francis Ford Coppola, Production Company Lucasfilm Ltd/Coppola Company, Time (original release): 110 mins, (re-release): 112 mins.

The Conversation (1974)

Starring Gene Hackman (*Harry Caul*), John Cazale (*Stan*), Allen Garfield (*Bernie Moran*), Frederic Forrest (*Mark*), Cindy Williams (*Ann*), Michael Higgins (*Paul*), Elizabeth MacRae (*Meredith*), Terri Garr (*Amy*), Harrison Ford (*Martin Stett*), Mark Wheeler (*Receptionist*), Robert Shields (*Mime*), Phoebe Alexander (*Lurleen*), Robert Duvall (*The Director*).
Directed by Francis Ford Coppola, Screenplay by Francis Ford Coppola, Photographed by Bill Butler, Edited by Walter Murch and Richard Chew, Music by David Shire, Produced by Francis Ford Coppola and Fred Roos, Production Company The Coppola Company/Paramount Pictures, Time: 113 mins.
On video through CIC Video: VHL/BEL 2051: 110 mins.

Dynasty (1976, TV Movie)

Starring Sarah Miles (*Jennifer Blackwood*), Stacey Keach (*Matt Blackwood*), Harris Yulin (*John Blackwood*), Harrison Ford (*Mark Blackwood*),

Tony Schwartz (*Harry Blackwood*), Amy Irving (*Amanda Blackwood*), Charles Weldon (*Sam Adams*), Stephanie Faulkner (*Lucinda*), Karmin Murcello (*Elvira*), John Carter (*Benjamin McCullum*), Sari Price (*Margaret McCullum*), Gerrit Graham (*Carver Blackwood*), Dennis Larson (*Mark, age 12*), Gary Lee Cooper (*Mark, age 6*).
Directed by Lee Philips, Teleplay by Sydney Carroll, based on the novel by James Michener, Produced by Buck Houghton, Production Company David Paradine TV Productions/Marjay Productions for NBC's *Saturday Night at the Movies*, Time: 99 mins.

Star Wars (1977)

Starring Mark Hamill (*Luke Skywalker*), Harrison Ford (*Han Solo*), Carrie Fisher (*Princess Leia Organa*), Peter Cushing (*Grand Moff Tarkin*), Sir Alec Guinness (*Ben "Obi-wan" Kenobi*), Anthony Daniels (*C-3PO*), Kenny Baker (*R2-D2*), Peter Mayhew (*Chewbacca*), David Prowse (*Lord Darth Vader*), Phil Brown (*Uncle Owen Lars*), Shelagh Fraser (*Aunt Beru Lars*), Jack Purvis (*Chief Jawa*), Biggs (*Dennis Lawson*).
Written and directed by George Lucas, Photographed by Gilbert Taylor, Edited by Paul Hirch, Marcia Lucas and Richard Chew, Production design by John Barry, Music by John Williams, Special effects supervisor John Dykstra, Sound effects by Ben Burtt, Production Supervisor Robert Watts, Produced by Gary Kurtz, Production Company Lucasfilm Ltd, Time: 121 mins.
On Video through CBS/Fox Video: 1052: 116 mins.

Heroes (1977)

Starring Henry Winkler (*Jack Dunne*), Sally Field (*Carol*), Harrison Ford (*Kenny Boyd*), Val Avery (*Bus Driver*), Olivia Cole (*Jan Adcox*), Hector Elias (*Dr Elias*), Dennis Burkley (*Gus*), Tony Burton (*Chef*), Michael Cavanaugh (*Peanuts*), Helen Craig (*Bus Depot Manager*), John P.Finnegan (*Mr Munro*), Betty McGuire (*Mrs Munro*), John O'Leary (*Ticket Clerk*), Tom Rosqui (*Second Patrolman*), Fred Struthman (*Nathan*), Caskey Swain (*Frank*), Earle Towne (*Leo Sturges*), Verna Bloom (*Waitress*), Kenneth Augustine (*Charles*), Rick Blanchard (*Andy*), Louis Carillo (*Stokes*), Robert Kretschman (*Robert*), Lee Cohn (*Patient*), Dick Ziker (*Artie*).
Directed by Jeremy Paul Kagan, Screenplay by James Carabatsos, Photographed by Frank Stanley, Edited by Patrick Kennedy, Music by Jack Nitzsche, Produced by David Foster and Lawrence Turman, Production Company Turman-Foster Company, Time 107 mins (cut from 113 mins).

Force 10 from Navarone (1978)

Starring Robert Shaw (*Major Mallory*), Harrison Ford (*Lieutenant-Colonel Mike Barnsby*), Barbara Bach (*Maritza Petrovitch*), Edward Fox (*Sergeant "Milly" Miller*), Franco Nero (*Captain Radicek*), Carl Wethers (*Sergeant Walter Weaver*), Richard Kiel (*Captain Drazak*), Alan Badel (*Major Petrovitch*), Angus MacInnes (*Lieutenant Doug Reynolds*), Michael Byrne (*Major Schroeder*), Philip Latham (*Commander Jensen*), Peter Buntic (*Lieutenant Marko*), Michael Sheard (*Sergeamt Bauer*), Leslie Schofield, Antony Langdon and Richard Hampton (*Interrogation Officers*), Paul Humpoletz (*Sergeant Bismark*), Dicken Ashworth (*Nolan*), Christopher Malcolm (*Rogers*), Nick Ellsworth (*Salvone*),

Jonathan Blake (*Oberstein*), Roger Owen (*Blake*), Frances Mughan, Mike Sirett, Graham Crowther and Jim Dowdall (*Force 10 Team*).
Directed by Guy Hamilton, Screenplay by Robin Chapman from a story by Carl Forman, based on a novel by Alistair MacLean, Photographed by Christopher Challis, Music by Ron Goodwin, Produced by Oliver A.Unger, Executive producer Carl Foreman, Production Company Navarone Productions, Time: 118 mins.
Announced by Columbia Video: never released.

Hanover Street (1979)

Starring Harrison Ford (*David Halloran*), Lesley-Anne Down (*Margaret Sellinger*), Christopher Plummer (*Paul Sellinger*), Alec McCowen (*Major Trumbo*), Richard Maur (*2nd Lt Jerry Cimino*), Michael Sacks (*2nd Lt Martin Hyer*), Patsy Kensit (*Sarah Sellinger*), Max Wall (*Harry Pike*), Shane Rimmer (*Col Ronald Bart*), Keith Buckley (*Lt Wells*), Sherrie Hewson (*Phyllis*), Cindy O'Callaghan (*Paula*), Di Trevis (*Elizabeth*) Suzanne Bertish (*French Girl*), Keith Alexander (*Soldier in Barn*), Jay Benedict (*Corp Daniel Giler*), John Ratzenberger (*Sgt John Lucas*), Eric Stine (*Farrell*), Hugh Frazer (*Capt Harold Lester*), William Hootkins (*Beef*).
Directed by Peter Hyams, Screenplay by Peter Hyams, Photographed by David Watkin, Edited by James Mitchell, Music by John Barry, Associate producers Michael Rachmil and Harry Benn, Produced by Paul N. Lazarus III, Executive producer Gordon G.T.Scott, Production Company Hanover Street Productions, Time: 108 mins.
On video through Columbia Video: CVT/CBT 10097: 105 mins.

The 'Frisco Kid (1979)

Starring Gene Wilder (*Avram Belinski*), Harrison Ford (*Tommy Lillard*), Rammon Bieri (*Mr Jones*), Val Bisloglio (*Chief Gray Cloud*), George Ralph DiCenzo (*Darryl Riggs*), Leo Fuchs (*Chief Rabbi*), Penny Peyser (*Rosalie*), William Smith (*Matt Diggs*), Jack Somack (*Samuel Bender*), Beege Barkett (*Sarah Mindl*), Shay Duffin (*O'Leary*), Walter Janowitz (*Old Amish Man*), Joe Kapp (*Monterano*), Clyde Kusatsu (*Mr Ping*), Cliff Pellow (*Mr Daniels*), Allan Rich (*Mr Bialik*), Henry Rowland (*1st Amish Farmer*), Vincent Schiavelli (*Brother Bruno*), John Steadman (*Booking Agent*), Ian Wolfe (*Father Joseph*), Steffen Zacharias (*Herschel Rosensheine*), Eda Reiss Medin (*Mrs Bender*), Tommy Lillard (*Sheriff*).
Directed by Robert Aldrich, Screenplay by Michael Elias and Frank Shaw, Photographed by Robert B.Hauser, Edited by Maury Winetrobe, Irving Rosenblum and Jack Horger, Music by Frank DeVol, Associate producer Melvin Dellar, Produced by Mace Neufeld, Executive producer Howard W.Koch Jr, Production Company Warner Bros, Time: 119 mins.
On video through Warner Home Video: WEV/WEX 61095: 118 mins.

The Empire Strikes Back (1980)

Starring Mark Hamill (*Luke Skywalker*), Harrison Ford (*Han Solo*), Carrie Fisher (*Princess Leia Organa*), Billy Dee Williams (*Lando Calrissian*), Anthony Daniels (*C-3PO*), Kenny Baker (*R2-D2*),

THE HARRISON FORD STORY

Peter Mayhew (*Chewbacca*), Frank Oz (*Yoda*), Sir Alec Guinness (*Ben "Obi-wan" Kenobi*), Jeremy Bulloch(*Boba Fett*), John Hollis(*Lando's Aide*), Jack Purvis(*Chief Ugnaught*), Des Webb(*Snow Creature*), Clive Revill (*Voice of the Emperor*), Kenneth Colley (*Admiral Piett*), Julian Glover (*General Veers*), Dennis Lawson(*Wedge*).

Directed by Irvin Kershner, Screenplay by Leigh Brackett and Lawrence Kasdan, from a story by George Lucas, Photographed by Peter Suschitsky, Production design by Norman Reynolds, Music by John Williams, Edited by Paul Hirsch, Special effects supervised by Brian Johnson and Richard Edlund, Associate producer Robert Watts, Produced by Gary Kurtz, Executive producer George Lucas, Production Company Lucasfilm Ltd, Time: 124 mins.

Raiders of the Lost Ark (1981)

Starring Harrison Ford(*Prof. Indiana Jones*), Karen Allen (*Marion Ravenwood*), Paul Freeman (*Belloq*), Ronald Lacey (*Toht*), John Rhys-Davies (*Sallah*), Denholm Elliot (*Brody*), Wolf Kahler (*Dietrich*), Anthony Higgins (*Gobler*), Alfred Molina (*Satipo*), Vic Tablian (*Barranca*), Don Fellows (*Col. Musgrove*), William Hootkins(*Maj Eaton*).

Directed by Steven Spielberg, Screenplay by Lawrence Kasdan, from a story by George Lucas and Philip Kaufman, Photographed by Douglas Slocombe, Production designed by Norman Reynolds, Music by John Williams, Edited by Michael Kahn, Visual Effects supervised by Richard Edlund, Associate producer Robert Watts, Produced by Frank Marshall, Executive producers George Lucas and Howard Kazanjian, Production Company Lucasfilm Ltd, Time: 115 mins. On video through CIC Video: VHR/BER 2076: 112 mins.

Blade Runner (1982)

Starring Harrison Ford (*Rick Deckard*), Rutger Hauer (*Roy Batty*), Sean Young (*Rachael*), Edward James Olmos (*Gaff*), M. Emmet Walsh (*Bryant*), Daryl Hannah (*Pris*), William Sanderson (*Sebastian*), Brion James (*Leon*), Joe Turkel (*Tyrell*), Joanna Cassidy (*Zhora*), James Hong (*Chew*), Morgan Paull (*Holden*), Kimiro Hiroshige (*Cambodian Lady*), Carolyn DeMirjian (*Saleslady*), Robert Ozkazaki (*Sushi Master*), Hy Pyke (*Taffy Lewis*), Kevin Thompson(*Bear*), John Edward Allen (*Kaiser*).

Directed by Ridley Scott, Screenplay by Hampton Fancher and David Peoples, based on the novel *Do Androids Dream of Electric Sheep* by Philip K.Dick, Photographed by Jordan Cronenweth, Production designed by Lawrence G.Paul, Music by Vangelis, Supervising editor Terry Rawlings, Special effects supervised by Douglas Trumbull, Richard Yuricich and David Dryer, Visual futurist Syd Mead, Associate producer Ivor Powell, Produced by Michael Deeley, Executive producers Brian Kelly and Hampton Fancher, Production Company The Blade Runner Partnership, Time: 114 mins. On Video through Warner Home Video: WEV/WEX 70008: 111 mins.

Return of the Jedi (1983)

Starring Mark Hamill (*Luke Skywalker*), Harrison Ford (*Han Solo*), Carrie Fisher (*Princess Leia Organa*), Billy Dee Williams (*Lando Calrissian*), Anthony Daniels (*C-3PO*), Peter Mayhew (*Chewbacca*), Sebastian Shaw (*Anakin Skywalker/Darth Vader*), David Prowse and Bob Anderson (*Darth Vader*), Ian McDiarmid(*The Emperor*), Frank Oz (*Yoda*), James Earl Jones (*voice of Darth Vader*), Sir Alec Guinness (*Ben "Obi-wan" Kenobi*), Jeremy Bulloch(*Boba Fett*).

Directed by Richard Marquand, Screenplay by Lawrence Kasdan, based on a story by George Lucas, Photographed by Alan Hume, Production designed by Norman Reynolds, Music by John Williams, Edited by Sean Barton, Marcia Lucas and Duwayne Dunham, Special visual effects by Dennis Muren, Ken Ralston and Richard Edlund, Makeup and creature design by Phil Tippett and Stuart Freeborn, Sound design by Ben Burtt, Co-produced by Robert Watts and Jim Bloom, Produced by Howard Kazanjian, Executive producer George Lucas, Production Company Lucasfilm Ltd, Time: 123 mins.

Indiana Jones and the Temple of Doom (1984)

Starring Harrison Ford (*Indiana Jones*) with Kate Capshaw. Directed by Steven Spielberg, Screenplay by Gloria Katz and Willard Huyck, based on a story by George Lucas, Photographed by Douglas Slocombe, Supervising editor Michael Kahn, Edited by Peter Pitt, Production designed by Elliot Scott, Special effects supervisor George Gibbs, Stunt arranger Vic Armstrong, Associate producer Kathleen Kennedy, Produced by Robert Watts, Executive producers George Lucas and Frank Marshall, Production Company Lucasfilm Ltd, Time: Not available at presstime.